Hello, My Name is Awesome

Adventures with Autism and the Almighty

Victoria Layne

Published by Mindstir Media, LLC
45 Lafayette Rd | Suite 181| North Hampton, NH 03862 | USA
1.800.767.0531 | www.mindstirmedia.com

Printed in the United States of America
ISBN-13: 979-8-9861392-3-4

To my mother, Stella.
I hope you have a front row view from heaven.

God thunders marvelously with His voice; He does great things which we cannot comprehend.

—Job 37:5 KJV

Introduction

The sound of silence isn't just the title of a classic Simon and Garfunkel song. The sound of silence was an everyday occurrence in my home for far too long. In a place where childish giggles, never-ending questions, and simple observations should abound, I woke daily to a deafening silence for which I constantly prayed a miracle.

While I was grateful for Atticus's ability to communicate through sign language and other gestures, I desperately wanted him to be able to speak words to communicate. During this trying time, I determined that if Atticus ever gained the ability to speak, I would document the words and stories that made me laugh, cry, or just touched my heart in a notable way.

Through God's faithfulness, and more work than I ever imagined would be required of me or Atticus, my beautiful boy began using recognizable language at the age of three years and three months. I soon amassed dozens of anecdotes, humorous interactions, and sweet, meaningful moments in our life together. The collection has continued to grow through the years.

When Atticus was six years old, we were eating lunch when he had a brief, but pivotal, interaction with a stranger. Atticus only spoke ten words, but those ten words set me on an unexpected and intimidating path. In that moment, I heard a voice—a voice so clear it was as if someone was sitting by my side. "That's the title of your book. Go write the book."

I had no intentions of turning my adventures with Atticus into a book. I was simply journaling because I wanted to save my child's words. He lingered in silence for what seemed an eternity while I anticipated a breakthrough. I was eternally grateful for every word. Perhaps I wanted the memories to last a lifetime. Perhaps, in the deep recesses of my mind, I was frightened he would lose the ability to talk again. Whatever the reason, I continued to record most events in a fervent manner without any intention of sharing them with the world, but the inner prodding wouldn't cease: "Write the book."

After a few years of ignoring the incessant call, I finally surrendered, and I sat down to write about my son and our life with autism. Our documented journey starts at the very beginning and continues through age eleven.

The following stories are some of my favorite—and not so favorite—moments I've shared with Atticus—amusing, challenging, charming, and at times, heartbreaking.

I hope you find the following pages to be all the above and so much more. I pray that if you are the parent of a child on the autism spectrum you will find hope and inspiration in our story. And if you are a parent of a typical-developing child, I pray you find understanding and compassion.

Chapter 1
Taking Charge

He's seven years old. As I sit in the church sanctuary, attending his first chapel performance, I watch him on stage singing about the fruit of the spirit—love, joy, peace, patience, kindness, goodness, faithfulness, gentleness, and self-control.

He attempts to dance and participate in childish, choreographed motions with forty other first graders. My heart races as I await his every move. The ensemble shifts into groups of four. They wrap their arms around each other and scrunch close together, symbolizing clusters of grapes.

I watch as he timidly takes part in a four-person squeeze, paying particular attention to his body language. His rigid movements make for an awkward performance. I can tell he's anxious and outside of his comfort zone. Despite his reservations and fears, he continues to move. He continues to sing.

I'm overwhelmed with gratitude, brimming with delight. Tears flood my eyes, blurring the scene in front of me. Try as I might, I can't stop the surge of emotion from rushing down my cheeks.

My mind drifts back to four years earlier when he participated in his first school performance at the tender age of three years and nine months. He attended a special-needs preschool in our school district. The program served children with a variety of disabilities—speech delays, autism, and Down Syndrome to name a few.

He experienced a meltdown a few minutes into the show. Overwhelmed by the crowd and noise, he sobbed and screamed while the other children sang. He looked terrified. His face turned bright red and tears covered his cheeks. I had a strong urge to rush the stage and pull him to safety—to relocate him into the comforting arms of his mommy—to assure him everything would be all right.

Before I could move, his teacher took him by the hand, sat him on her lap, and continued to lead the rest of the children in song. I was touched with her care for him and thankful her soothing touch slowly calmed him.

He's come a long way since that day. We've come a long way.

My mind snaps back to present day as students take turns speaking into a microphone. They present an oral explanation about the fruit of the Spirit after each song.

A couple of children appear to struggle with the reading of their planned remarks. A few speak in hushed tones so that you barely hear what they are saying. Others mumble as they speak, and several are well spoken.

Eventually it's his turn—my Atticus—my precious, beautiful, miracle from God who has overcome so much in his short life.

My heartbeat thunders in my ears as he approaches the microphone. Without hesitation, he delivers his lines: "Patience is the next one. I'm sure we know what this means. Have you ever been told to have patience? The patience God is talking about is for those little things like waiting to open your Christmas presents, but it also means to be patient for answers to prayers that might take years to be answered."

He's clear. He's powerful. He's articulate.

I exhale and collect my thoughts. *Yes, he will make a fine public speaker one day. Perhaps he can develop the speaking skills to be president as he often expresses a desire to be someday.*

Once again, I'm overwhelmed as memories rush back to a time in our lives when I didn't know if he would ever speak.

Sometimes our beginning seems like so long ago, but seven years isn't that long ago. It seems as though it was only yesterday.

***

Atticus was born on a steamy, hot August morning. Everyone expected a nine- to ten-pound baby, but from the beginning, he wasn't anything like we expected. He only weighed seven pounds, thirteen ounces.

I had an uneventful pregnancy, but delivery didn't go as anticipated.

Hello, My Name Is Awesome

My planned natural birth morphed into a nightmare of induced labor and a mixture of pharmaceutical drugs.

My water broke early one Wednesday morning, but I didn't go into active labor. I stayed home for hours hoping to induce contractions using various natural methods—walking, massage, and raspberry tea. Nothing worked. With no labor pains in sight, I reluctantly went to the hospital late that afternoon. Because the amniotic sac had already ruptured, the medical staff said they needed to induce labor immediately. But I insisted they allow more time for contractions to happen naturally.

After several hours of walking hallways and climbing stairs, the nurse midwife convinced me to submit to induction. Upon checking my vitals, my temperature read 99 degrees. Because of the slight rise in temperature, she said I needed an antibiotic on top of the induction medication already in use. I declined several times, but the nurse midwife refused to take no for an answer. She summoned the on-call doctor, who administered scare tactics, to bully me into the decision they wanted me to make.

My mother was present in the room, and she played right into their fear approach, which came just short of promising an infection that could result in all sorts of terrible problems for the baby. My mother choked back tears as she strained to tell me I needed to do as the medical professionals instructed. My husband stood idly by without a word of support.

I couldn't battle by myself any longer. I was in a vulnerable state with no strong voice to stand up for me, support or defend my decisions, and no one to encourage me. Step-by-step my hope for a natural, drug-free delivery collapsed into the dustbin of tarnished dreams.

Hours later, my drug-induced nightmare was topped off with four hours of pushing before the doctor was brought in to perform a vacuum extraction. Thankfully, the first attempt was successful, and my perfect, beautiful baby boy made his appearance into this world with bright eyes and an immediate sense of curiosity.

He was extremely alert and aware of his surroundings. He spent the first three-and-a-half hours of his life gazing around the room, following movements, reacting to sounds, and producing little chirping sounds.

The new experience didn't seem out of the ordinary to me, but the nurses made comments about his alertness. "He's an active one," said one nurse. "He's very observant," said another. I considered his liveliness to be normal, but they told me babies don't typically stay awake that long right after birth. This child of mine had no interest in sleep; it seemed he was already eager to explore the world.

As I sat in the hospital bed, recovering from the painful events of the past fourteen hours, I marveled at the miracle I held—so perfect, so beautiful, so scary. *Why was I entrusted to care for this child? How would I be successful?*

For several years leading up to Atticus's birth, I adopted a natural and organic approach to living and eating. Giving birth had been a lifelong fear, but in recent years, I had grown to embrace the natural process and the prospect of childbirth. I possessed a true sense of peace throughout my pregnancy. I realized what an amazing miracle God allowed me to be a part of, and I was thankful to experience the glory of it all. God fully equipped my body to birth a child. I had no fear. But as I sat in the hospital bed staring at Atticus, I felt overpowered by the seven-pound baby I cradled in my arms—so new, so small. Did I possess the nurturing skills necessary for his wellbeing?

I intended to breastfeed my son, but much like my hope for a natural childbirth, breastfeeding didn't go as planned either. Atticus struggled with attachment from the beginning. The lactation nurse spent a generous amount of time with us, coaching me and trying to get Atticus to latch on during his first day of life outside the womb. We thought we achieved success late that evening, but the struggle continued, so I reluctantly gave him a small amount of formula before getting some rest that night.

After we left the hospital, I continued to try to breastfeed. But after two weeks of weak attachment by him, screaming fits of hunger minutes after I thought he had been fully fed, several visits to a lactation specialist, and producing only an ounce or two of milk each time I used a breast pump, the experience became an exercise in futility and frustration. My body wasn't producing enough milk to properly feed my child, and he refused to properly attach. We were each other's enemy it seemed.

With an anguished heart, I stopped trying to breastfeed and drove to the store to stock up on baby formula. I was devastated that I couldn't natu-

Hello, My Name Is Awesome

rally provide food for my child, and I was jealous of those women who could.

Shortly after Atticus began a full-time feeding regimen of store-bought formula, he began experiencing what the doctor termed *reflux*, and he regularly battled constipation. The thought that he was just a few weeks old and dealing with digestive issues concerned me and gave me more reason to beat myself up over my inability to breastfeed.

I was apprehensive about using processed formula from the beginning, but I honestly didn't realize I had any other choice. So to prevent my baby from starving to death, I dutifully went to the store each week for a new supply.

His battle with constipation was terrible to witness. He struggled to have a bowel movement every three or four days, and his attempts inevitably resulted in a few marble-sized, hard pellets each time.

I called the doctor's office to discuss my worries with the nurse. She instructed me to put a teaspoon of prune juice in his formula once a day. The juice helped things move a little smoother, but when I stopped using it, the marble-sized pellets reappeared.

When I took Atticus into the office for a checkup, I voiced my concerns to his pediatrician. The doctor told me it's normal for babies to go three days without a bowel movement and then provided the same prune juice advice. *Am I supposed to give my baby prune juice every day of his life indefinitely?*

I also discussed the enormous amount of formula that Atticus regurgitated after each feeding. The doctor told me that was normal as well. *It may be normal in today's America, but it certainly isn't the way our bodies were intended to work.*

No one—babies, children, or adults—should go three or four days without a bowel movement. A little spit up once in a while is normal for babies, but regurgitating half of the bottle every time he fed shouldn't be considered normal and isn't the way our systems should run.

These two issues weighed heavily on my mind the first few months of Atticus's life. Unfortunately, I was at a loss as to what to do about the situation. My thought process was stuck. *If only I could breastfeed him, he wouldn't have to deal with these problems.* That mindset only made it harder for me to think logically.

Why doesn't anyone think these issues are a problem except me?

I came to a crossroad when Atticus was six months old. I continued to complain, mostly to my mother, about his digestive health. His body was not processing food in a beneficial manner. He continued struggling with constipation, and reflux was a never-ending battle of ruined bibs and filthy clothes.

Then, one Friday evening, Atticus was lying on the living room floor, when a geyser erupted from his belly, spewing vomit straight up in the air. I watched as the clear liquid cascaded to the ground—all over the brand-new carpet. I had reached my limit. In that moment, I became determined to find an alternative to the manufactured formula he had been consuming the first six months of his life.

Finally, I listened to my gut—not other people. I knew fresh, whole foods were the answer to my wellness, so why wouldn't the same nutritional principles apply to my baby? I scoured the Internet that evening, looking for answers. At the time, alternative recipes were not easy to come by. I spent hours searching through website after website, chasing ideas that went down one rabbit hole after another. One link led to another link that led to yet another.

My brain gathered a ton of material and scrambled to retain the knowledge. I absorbed information regarding babies, proper nutrition, goat's milk versus cow's milk, and vitamin and mineral deficiencies. I discovered several sites warning against manufactured baby formulas. I found myself agreeing with them because I had been living with the results of feeding my child the product for the last six months.

One topic I kept running across was using goat's milk as an alternative to cow's milk. I read how goat's milk is more easily digested and matches the human body better than cow's milk. I was sold, but I had little desire to use a powder mixture from a can.

I continued to search into the wee hours of the night until I found a website that listed a homemade formula using goat's milk. A grandmother, who suspected her grandson was suffering from a nutritional deficiency, concocted the recipe. After watching her grandchild thrive while using the new formula, she posted the recipe online hoping to help others who found themselves in a similar situation. I admit I was nervous, but I was deter-

Hello, My Name Is Awesome

mined, and it all made perfect sense to me.

I decided I wanted to find someone else who may have used this recipe. I began searching message boards for what seemed an eternity. I feared I wouldn't find anyone, and then it happened. On an obscure parenting website, I found a single message from a woman living in the northeastern part of America who had mentioned using the very same recipe for her son.

I sent her a private message explaining my situation and asked her how the formula worked for her family. She responded the following morning with the news I was hoping for—she loved the formula! She began using the recipe when her first son was a few months old, and the difference in his health and energy level was night and day. After seeing the impact of the formula in her firstborn, she used the same formula with her second child from birth, and he was flourishing as well.

It was now Sunday morning, roughly thirty-eight hours since I resolved to change Atticus's nutritional input. I was fully committed to following my instincts and giving my child the healthiest food I could provide him. I drove to a health-food store with my ingredients list in hand and bought all the necessary items—my first real act of taking control of my son's health.

When Atticus woke up Monday morning, I took him downstairs to the kitchen where I made my first batch of homemade baby formula. Into the blender went various ingredients that included, among other things, goat's milk, several liquid vitamins and minerals, and one of the most significant and beneficial items that aided in his digestive recovery, probiotics.

I handed his bottle to him and anxiously watched for his reaction to the new taste in his mouth. As it turned out, I didn't have any need to worry. Atticus loved his new food. After he finished eating, I watched and waited. I waited for his bib to be covered with formula like it had been every other day prior. It didn't happen.

Proper nutrition made a huge difference.

With just a change from manufactured formula to a homemade formula of goat's milk chock-full of vitamins, minerals, and probiotics—Atticus went from regurgitating half of his formula each feeding to a little spit up every few feedings. He went from producing marble-sized balls of waste every three to four days to experiencing one or two healthy bowel movements every single day.

His young, vulnerable body was finally functioning in a way that made sense to me—the way God designed it to function. He seemed to thrive. His energy level increased dramatically within the first couple of days. He became more active and alive. His eyes sparkled. The transformation was truly astonishing to witness. I knew I had made the right decision for him. I was relieved I no longer had to worry about the food I was putting in his body. But little did I know that my worries were far from over.

Chapter 2
Silence

Atticus met all the milestones of typical childhood development. He was a champion at rolling, sitting, standing, and walking. Vocalization began early with an abundance of cooing at two months of age. As he grew, his sounds progressed to outbursts of laughter and loud, vigorous, ear-piercing squeals that made you wish you were hard of hearing. Months of babbling ensued, followed by the definitive sounds of "Dada" and "I di I di" at fourteen months.

When Atticus was a few weeks old, I read an article about teaching babies to use sign language. *That's a grand idea!* So when he turned nine months old, I began using simple signs while interacting with him. I was hopeful that he would connect the words to the hand gestures so our communication could flourish early. Atticus didn't let me down. At twelve months old, he used his first unprompted sign during breakfast one morning. He signed, "More." I was beyond thrilled! A few weeks later, he delighted me once again when he used multiple signs to say, "More milk please."

He was soon using several signs to communicate his needs, including eat, food, water, milk, book, please, thank you, mommy, daddy, and finished.

"Finished" was his favorite sign. Whenever he didn't want to do something, he puckered his lips, scrunched his face, and emphatically signed, *"Finished!"*

If he didn't want to be with a certain person, he signed, *"Finished!"*

If he didn't want to read a certain book, he signed, *"Finished!"*

If he didn't want to leave the house, he signed, *"Finished!"*

He was forceful with the use of that particular sign. He was serious, and he let everyone around him know. I found it comical.

Atticus continued to learn and use more than sixty signs as time went on. I will forever be grateful for the inner prompting to teach him sign language. At the time I made the decision, I had no clue how valuable his ability to communicate with his hands would be to him, and to me, in our future.

When Atticus was sixteen months old, we went Christmas shopping one chilly December evening. After we finished browsing the store aisles and purchasing gifts to put under our tree, we walked to our car. I loaded Atticus into his car seat while his dad pushed the cart across the parking lot toward the corral. As he watched his father walk away, Atticus said, "See ya, Dada!"

His words made me smile. *He's going to start using real words and having real conversations!* Atticus babbled, squealed, and shrieked a lot, but he didn't really say any intelligible words other than "Dada" and "I di, I di," so, "See ya, Dada," was the breakthrough I had been waiting for.

In that moment of rejoicing, I never dreamed they would be the final words he attempted to speak before our world went silent.

Up to this point, I wasn't too concerned about Atticus's development. Was he different from the so-called "typical" one year old running around? Yes.

He spent a generous amount of time each day looking through books and magazines rather than playing with toys. He had an intense interest in the alphabet, numbers, and street signs. We couldn't visit a Meijer grocery store without walking to the stop sign near the entrance. Every single time we exited the store, he would point to the sign and scream if I didn't pay attention to his pointing. Then I had to push the cart over to the sign where he pointed to the word until I read "stop" aloud. He then flapped his hands and smiled from excitement over hearing the word. I knew he wasn't like other children his age.

While his fascination with numbers, letters, signs, and books probably wasn't what anyone considered normal, I wasn't concerned about it. I did suspect, however, that autism might be a factor due to some of his other behaviors.

He developed an obsession with ceiling fans at an early age, and his fascination didn't dissipate with time.

Hand flapping from excitement, anxiety, or sadness emerged just be-

Hello, My Name Is Awesome

fore his first birthday.

He wouldn't let anyone read to him except me.

He had a peculiar fascination with an eight-count box of crayons. He liked to pull each crayon out of the box and hand them to me one by one. I had to stand each one on their flat ends. Once all eight crayons were standing in a straight line, Atticus put them back in the box. We repeated the process several times a day for several months.

When Atticus was fifteen months old, I was preparing a Thanksgiving Day meal that triggered the smoke detector. The blaring, beeping sound resulted in a massive meltdown that we didn't know how to handle. Atticus screamed and wailed at the sound of the noise. His body grew rigid. His pained expression showed suffering. Nothing we did could calm his emotional and physical turmoil. We didn't understand why he reacted so violently to that sound. Once we managed to silence the alarm, his screaming stopped, but he continued to cry and breathe heavily. It took several minutes to calm his shaking body and alleviate his fear. That holiday incident made it perfectly clear that he had sensory problems with certain sounds.

Atticus liked to take car rides on the freeway. He loved to point to the green freeway signs and was overjoyed if I read them to him as he pointed. Because of his intense interest in the signs, I always wondered if he could read the words himself. But he didn't talk, so I didn't know.

We usually took the same route when returning home from the grocery store, but if I decided to take a different exit than I typically used, he would become upset. He would reach for the exit sign as we drove by and cry the rest of the way home. I later learned that his conduct stemmed from the rigid behaviors and love of routine displayed by autistic children.

Atticus experienced a meltdown that I will never forget. He was a little over a year old at the time and couldn't verbalize his emotions. This usually didn't present a problem because he had been on an eating and sleeping schedule since he was a few weeks old, so he knew what to expect most days. He was a delightful toddler who typically only cried when physically hurting.

On this particular evening, Atticus was happily looking at a book when dinnertime arrived. I took the book from his hands and told him it was time to eat. He began to cry. At first, his actions reminded me of a spoiled child who acts up to get his way. Since I was determined to never play that game, I told him to stop crying and go to the kitchen and eat. He didn't stop. Atticus continued his emotional meltdown for more than two hours with loud, painful, shrill cries complete with tears, red face, and trembling lips. He also moaned and whimpered as he lay limp on the floor. Occasionally, he lofted tongue trills, which sounded like anger boiling out of his mouth, while he sat on his ankles flicking the carpet with his fingers.

The incessant, alternating range of emotions made me feel powerless. If I tried to speak to him, his mood intensified. Unable to stop the irrational feelings that poured out of him, I quickly learned to let him be. But the never-ending onslaught of emotion horrified me.

I felt a deep desire to run away from home—to escape what my life had become. The longer he continued his outbursts, the more discouraged I became. In that moment of turmoil, I was confident I didn't possess the skills, the empathy, or the heart required to be this child's mother.

Was all of this really over a book?

After nearly two and a half hours, Atticus finally walked over to me— his weary and bewildered mother. He let out an exhausted breath and buried his head in my lap, bringing an end to this unexpected, dreadful ordeal.

Now, after all those early signs, Atticus's sudden silence was the biggest red flag of all. I should have been more concerned, but despite all the rigid and repetitive behaviors, emerging sensory problems, unconventional interests, and now speech regression, Atticus was a happy, intelligent, and engaging child. He seemed to understand my every word, and he communicated masterfully through pointing and sign language. When he lost eye contact with me, I would cup his little cheeks in my hands and tell him to, "Look Mommy in the eyes." I had read that autistic children avoid eye contact, and I never wanted to lose that connection with him, so I encouraged contact often.

The fact that Atticus met his early milestones and appeared unusually bright caused me to neglect his weaknesses early on.

When he was seventeen months old, he wanted me to read his favorite book. I don't know why, but instead of reading to him, I asked, "Atticus, do you know where the word 'zoo' is? Can you point to the word 'zoo'?"

    Hello, My Name Is Awesome

He looked at me; his brilliant blue eyes grew wide as he smiled. Excitement radiated from my son as he looked down at the book and pointed to the word "zoo."

I couldn't believe what happened. I asked, "How did you do that?" fully expecting an answer but knowing he couldn't provide one.

He smiled, quite pleased with himself and my response. He knew he had impressed me.

I telephoned my mother and asked her if it was possible for a seventeen-month-old child to recognize words. Then I recapped the events that just transpired. My mother was silent with disbelief. Then she reiterated what she had told me many times prior to this particular phone call and said, "I'm telling you that boy's a genius." I wasn't convinced he was a genius, but I was certain he wasn't common.

Moments like this allowed me to spend an enormous amount of time focusing on Atticus's positive traits. Rarely did I contemplate the negatives. Still, I felt his loss of spoken words should be addressed.

At his eighteen-month checkup, I casually told the pediatrician that Atticus wasn't trying to talk. I intentionally left out that I believed he was autistic. I didn't want to haggle with doctors or have that information in Atticus's medical file. At the time, my only goal was to find out what my next step should be.

The doctor provided contact information for Early Intervention. I had never heard of such a program, but I took the information. I was hesitant to make the call, but after weighing my options, it became obvious this was the best course of action for the wellbeing of our family, so I called a few days later.

The only thing that mattered to me was getting help for Atticus. I knew the sooner we started working on the problem, the better our results would be. From the day he was born, I strived to make wise decisions. If something concerned me, I was proactive in my search for a solution. My heart ached with devotion. I couldn't allow myself to relax or believe issues would resolve on their own.

The Bible tells us that "The soul of the sluggard desireth, and hath nothing: but the soul of the diligent shall be made fat." Proverbs 13:4 (KJV).

I realized I had spent a lifetime participating in slothful and sluggish behavior, hoping for a desired outcome but neglecting the work required to achieve it. The secret, ambitious dreams of my childhood faded as I grew into a timid, lonely teen. As a full-grown woman, I was riddled with social anxiety and paralyzed by fear. My early dreams weren't just a dying ember, they were now a cold pile of ashes containing fundamental pieces of my heart and youthful aspirations for brighter tomorrows.

I couldn't allow that to happen to Atticus.

With no time to waste, I determined to be diligent. I poured my heart into giving him hope for brighter tomorrows. The first step was to hear him speak again. I vowed to make phone calls and attend meetings. I'd perform the work. I wouldn't rest. I had a desired outcome for my child, so I prayed without ceasing, faithfully believing God for a miracle and waiting for Atticus to be "made fat."

Chapter 3
Getting to Work

When Atticus was twenty months old, we began working with professionals from Early Intervention. After the initial red tape and paperwork, we received home visits by an early intervention specialist.

The specialist reviewed our personal information and asked me the same questions on each visit. She always spent a few minutes blowing bubbles while interacting with Atticus, and then she left. I never understood the point of those early visits unless the aim was to test my patience for the monotonous process.

She eventually made a referral to a speech language pathologist. *Finally!* To my relief, we began working with a speech therapist named Csaga the month Atticus turned two.

I've proclaimed on more than one occasion that God has always put the right people in our lives when Atticus needed them most. Csaga was no exception. Not only was she a speech therapist, but she had intimate knowledge and understanding of autism as well. She was a great resource.

Throughout the following year, she challenged me, I questioned her, and she made it her mission to make sure I understood the importance of being proactive in my approach to Atticus's development and wellbeing. She was adamant I always be prepared to advocate for him in all areas of life.

Csaga visited our home once a month to conduct home-based speech therapy sessions. During the hour-long appointments, she took notes as we discussed my son's progress, or lack thereof, since her previous visit. She interacted with Atticus by talking and reading books to him, hoping to evoke imitative sounds. In the beginning, Atticus resisted Csaga's attempts to read to him, always grabbing the book and handing it to me. He was insistent in his desire to hear Mommy's familiar tone. But she stood firm, and he eventually adjusted to the change.

At the end of each session, Csaga handed me a written outline of therapies she wanted me to utilize until her next home visit. She always included a list of books I was to read to Atticus several times throughout the month. I was instructed to use gestures and pause often to see if he would respond.

We read simple books, such as *Doggies*, to try to elicit imitative sounds from him. *Doggies* was one of his favorite books. Each page depicted a new dog with different shapes, sizes, and barks—the large, aggressive dog with the deep, loud *WOOF!* The tiny, white, furry dog with the high-pitched *yap*. Atticus loved my interpretation of each dog and wanted me to read the book regularly. While he didn't talk or attempt to use words at the time, he occasionally tried to imitate animals, but he rarely had success producing the correct sounds.

We also read books like *Chicka Chicka Boom Boom* for the fun phonics involved. Atticus loved books, so this part of therapy was easy. His smile and full attention told me he enjoyed listening to my exaggerated presentations and watching my boisterous demeanor during our readings.

Another speech therapy strategy I implemented was using simple language with him. So instead of saying, "Atticus, put on your shoes," I was to simply say, "Shoes on." This was more difficult than one would expect. When you're used to talking in complete sentences, it can seem like a herculean task to use less syllables. I often had to correct myself. I had to be intentional with every single word I said to him. I felt like I was changing who I was in order to communicate in a way that would benefit him. The more involved I became with his therapy, the more isolated I felt.

Other than the professionals I was working with, I was fighting this battle alone. While Atticus's father, Tim, was present in our lives, he was not involved in any aspect of our son's therapies. He seemed unfazed that his son suffered delays in many areas, including speech.

Tim didn't mind being the dad who babysits or takes his child out for dinner and fun, but he showed no interest in the possibility of his son being autistic—or what that meant for our lives. So, any type of home therapy was hoisted broadly on my shoulders. All decisions for Atticus's future were

Hello, My Name Is Awesome

in my hands. Tim's emotional distance stung, and the loneliness I felt was suffocating.

My solitary existence couldn't prevent me from doing everything within my power to help my child. When I was instructed to repeat every word I said to Atticus, I did so: "Shoes on! Shoes on!" When I was given certain sounds like "ba-ba and dee-dee" to say to him several times per day, I modelled them and allowed him time to repeat. When I was told to exaggerate words such as *oops*, which became *ooooooooops*, I complied. All these simple sounds were challenging for Atticus. In the beginning, he didn't repeat much of anything except the dog sounds, but as time went on, he began to attempt some of them. Sadly, he often produced incorrect consonant and/or vowel sounds when he tried.

Csaga recommended pretend play with Little People toys and barnyard animal figures to give Atticus a chance to communicate through pretend play. I bought both, but Atticus had little interest in playing with them or attempting dialogue of any kind.

I spent hours with Atticus each week repeating the multiple therapies on our to-do list and begging him to repeat my silly sounds. He was always willing to read, and since a big part of the treatment involved books, it wasn't hard to keep him interested in that portion of his therapy. But attempting to talk didn't come easy for him.

A couple of months into working with Csaga, she recommended that Atticus be evaluated by an occupational therapist (OT). Her suggestion was baffling. *Why does he need to be evaluated? He's perfectly fine outside of his lack of speech.* But she was concerned with his motor planning abilities and strongly advised an OT evaluation.

She explained that motor-planning delays can affect a person's fine and gross motor skills. Likewise, she was concerned with Atticus's sensory processing abilities because sensory problems also affect motor planning due to the inability to absorb and process outside stimuli. Her professional eye obviously saw things my untrained eye couldn't see.

I mentioned to Csaga that we had experienced several choking incidents involving Atticus. He stuffed his mouth, didn't chew food correctly, and he sometimes left food in his mouth for long periods of time before swallowing. Because of these issues, the OT wanted to observe his eating, so she decided to make her first visit during lunch. She conducted a thorough assessment a few days later.

Once the evaluation was complete, the OT and I sat on my living room floor while she told me all about my two-year-old child.

She used a lot of unfamiliar language that confused me. She told me Atticus's fine motor skills were delayed, that he had low muscle tone, delayed motor planning, a dysfunctional vestibular system, and used other foreign terms like proprioceptive and tactile senses. She supplied numerous handouts, with information regarding the new language, which made my head spin when I read them.

I was at a loss as to what all these things meant and had a terrible time grasping the details. The one thing I realized, however, was they all added up to her telling me my child was broken. My heart ached at the realization of what she was saying to me.

Before the OT left that day, she gave us a plastic, vibrating alligator that Atticus was to use to massage the inside of his mouth. This was supposed to stimulate the oral area. I was told to start using an electric toothbrush on him for the same reason. He gladly chewed the alligator, but he didn't respond to the quivering object hammering against his cheeks and gums. It was as if his mouth didn't sense the presence of the electronic gadget. I was also instructed to use lemons and limes to "wake up his mouth" with strong flavors. He finally had a reaction when I gave him pieces of the tart fruits. When he closed his eyes and scrunched his face, I knew the sour citrus fruits were doing their job.

The OT provided a list of several exercises to help with Atticus's oral problems. He was to blow bubbles, but since he couldn't blow air through his mouth at will, he couldn't complete the task. He was to suck applesauce through a straw, but he struggled with that as well, unable to move the thick substance out of the cup and through the tube. He was to start playing a kazoo, but he couldn't figure out how to produce any sound from it either.

Is my child truly broken? Are other toddlers able to do these things? I had no idea, but I wasn't going to concern myself with other toddlers. All I knew was Atticus and I had a long road ahead of us, and success was going to take

Hello, My Name Is Awesome

a lot of effort on both our parts.

The OT returned to our home once a month for therapy sessions. Like the speech therapist, at the end of each session she left me a list of therapies and exercises to implement and practice until her next visit.

Now I was playing full-time speech therapist and occupational therapist for my child. I didn't complain though. I was determined to do everything they suggested to help Atticus succeed.

Before long, the OT recommended that Atticus be evaluated by a physical therapist (PT). She was concerned about his gross motor skills. The PT's evaluation discovered weak core muscles, poor balance, and the need to improve skills such as pedaling a tricycle. We hit the trifecta!

Sometime during our home-based speech sessions, Csaga suggested that Atticus be tested for autism. I knew her concern was valid, but I was reluctant to have him tested. Even though I had believed for quite a while that he was autistic, I didn't feel a diagnosis was necessary. Csaga disagreed, and upon each visit, she continued to gently urge me to have him tested. Finally, I agreed.

Once the Autism Diagnostic Observation Schedule (ADOS) assessment was complete, I received the results from the administering psychologist.

Her report concluded that while Atticus engaged in some stereotypical behaviors during testing, he didn't meet the criteria for autism or any other diagnosis. I was somewhat surprised and relieved at the same time.

While reading the report, I paid particular attention to the psychologist's remarks. She noted that Atticus responded consistently to his name, made appropriate eye contact, relied mostly on nonverbal strategies such as facial expressions and gestures to communicate, and that he clearly appeared to enjoy his interactions with the examiner.

Although he was largely nonverbal at the time of testing, his ability to communicate without using intelligible words was strong. I believe his enormous strength in this area was the main contributor to the outcome of the testing. Even at the tender age of two years and ten months, Atticus had many strengths, but he also displayed numerous weaknesses. Much like myself, his strengths made it easy for people to overlook his weaknesses.

Still, my child was free from an autism diagnosis, and that made me happy.

We worked with the therapists from Early Intervention for a year. During our time together, Atticus progressed from using sign language and other gestures for communication, to verbally using one- to two-word phrases. However, most of his words were difficult to understand due to his inability to produce the correct consonant or vowel sound. He continued to use sign language and other gestures to communicate, but at least he was attempting to speak. I was thankful for his progress over the course of a year.

Upon Atticus's third birthday, he aged out of the Early Intervention program and transitioned into a special-needs preschool in our district. The therapists from Early Intervention oversaw the testing that had to take place in order to qualify Atticus for the preschool program.

The Multi-factored Evaluation (MFE) consisted of several tests administered by the speech language pathologist, the occupational therapist, the physical therapist, the early intervention specialist, and the psychologist.

The test results found, among other things, that Atticus exhibited, "Significant delays in auditory comprehension and expressive communication, and a severe delay/disorder in his phonological system effecting his overall ability to communicate with others." That was just the speech portion.

All told, his educational needs in the preschool setting were summarized in his Individual Education Plan (IEP) as needing:

- Improved oral-motor functioning for speech production
- Improved language comprehension and expression
- Improved social communication skills
- Improved motor planning skills
- Improved sensory integrative foundations for learning

After our final home-based therapy session was complete, Csaga asked if I would keep her updated on Atticus and his future progress. She expressed how much she enjoyed working with him, and she believed he had a ton of potential. She communicated that she had never witnessed a child experience such progress while working with Early Intervention. She praised me for my active involvement, the role I took in every suggested therapy, and my determination to help Atticus succeed.

I needed to hear her words of confirmation and encouragement. I was fighting a lonely battle, so her words gave me hope and reinforced that I was doing the right thing for him.

Csaga reiterated that I'm Atticus's advocate, and no matter what, I must stand strong and be willing to fight for what I know is right where he is concerned. She emphasized that I should always remember that no one knows my child better than me. This seemed to be extremely important for her to make me understand.

Csaga's influence in those early days is solely responsible for the way I handle any conflict that may arise to this day. I will always be grateful that she crossed our path and was part of our journey.

Atticus and I were now ready to begin a new chapter in our life in the way of special- needs preschool. We would leave our familiar group of professionals to begin working with an entire new group of strangers.

I was uncertain of what was in store, but I had peace. I rested in the belief that God would tend to my son's every need. I believed in my heart that his future held endless possibilities despite his early struggles.

God's Word proclaims, "For I know the thoughts that I think toward you, saith the LORD, thoughts of peace, and not of evil, to give you an expected end. Then shall ye call upon me, and ye shall go and pray unto me, and I will hearken unto you. And ye shall seek me, and find me, when ye shall search for me with all your heart." Jeremiah 29:11-13.

This promise was made to the Israelites who were banished into Babylon for seventy years. With these words, God gave his people an assurance of hope for a brighter future. I hadn't been exiled to a foreign land, but I felt like my life had taken a tumultuous turn into the unknown. At times I felt lost, confused, and alone. My once simple world was spinning in an alien direction, and I was helplessly adrift in all the commotion. I had to learn a new language. I had to familiarize myself with a system I wanted no part of. I had a child who I knew was autistic. Despite the non-diagnosis, I was living in the land of autism—and I knew it. Still, I had peace.

I knew where my hope lived. I knew where my help came from. I prayed fervently to a God who I know delivered His people from bondage, and that very same God anchored me and gave me hope that my child would have a bright and successful future no matter the odds.

I continued to have faith that He was leading us in the direction we should go.

Hello, My Name Is Awesome

Chapter 4
Preschool and Monkey Milk

Atticus qualified for special-needs preschool based on a severe communication delay, but he continued to receive occupational therapy due to delayed motor planning and sensory needs.

The preschool program was geared toward children with special needs but also accepted several typical developing children as peer models. Each class in the district was led by a licensed teacher/intervention specialist who, in our case, had several years of experience in the special-needs classroom setting. The classes were small, usually ten to fifteen students, supervised by a teacher, a teacher's assistant, and an extra aide if a child required additional support, which Atticus did.

Our family couldn't afford the therapies Atticus required, so I agreed to the special-needs preschool program because I knew it was a way for him to continue receiving the therapies he desperately needed. The only difference would be he now had access to a licensed speech therapist and occupational therapist on a weekly basis, instead of once a month. I continued to practice the therapies at home that I had learned throughout the year working with Early Intervention, but hope reigned in my heart because my son was receiving professional services every week.

I also agreed to the program because typical developing children were included in the class. I was adamant that regular children surround Atticus in all aspects of life. I was convinced he would never live up to his potential and overcome certain obstacles if he wasn't given the same opportunities as, and surrounded by, typical children.

Special-needs preschool runs concurrent with the normal school year calendar, so Atticus entered the program on his third birthday.

I was somewhat anxious his first day as I imagine any parent would be. I was about to leave my child in unfamiliar surroundings and entrust his care to a group of people I didn't know. Also, Atticus couldn't talk to me about anything. *How would I know what happened to him during our time apart?* The thought stretched my nerves taut. No matter how much I tried to remain optimistic, scenarios no parent wants to consider raced through my mind.

Making our way from the parking lot to the school building that first day, Atticus, as usual, remained silent. I held his hand and gently talked to him about what to expect. I tried to reassure him that he would have fun. I let him know that we would walk into the school building together, he would stay with his teacher, and then mommy would leave.

The closer we got to the large, one-story, brick building, the tighter he squeezed my hand.

Once inside, we met his teacher, Mrs. P. She seemed pleasant enough with a ready smile and an upbeat, lively personality. This was not the school I toured, or the teacher I met, when I first considered a move to the preschool program. This school and teacher had a much friendlier vibe than the other, and I immediately sensed both were a better fit for Atticus.

Mrs. P's classroom was large, orderly, and freshly designed for the new school year. Neatly written names labeled wall hooks where the children would hang their book bags and coats. Clean tables with small chairs sat in the middle of the room awaiting the arrival of several tiny tots. A white board hung on the wall with a colorful blue rug lying below it on the floor. Several bins full of supplies lined a wall. A chart, with student names crisply written on one side, stood alone, waiting for a picture to be placed beside the name. I was impressed with the organization of her room.

As I struggled to say goodbye, Mrs. P. did her best to assure me everything would be fine. Atticus remained silent throughout our discussion. He stood beside us looking terrified and clinging tightly to my hand. When the time came to say goodbye, I hugged and kissed my baby one last time before turning him over to his first teacher. Then I exited the building.

The school day was only two hours and forty minutes long, but it seemed like an eternity. I couldn't wait to pick up Atticus and hear all about his first day.

Hello, My Name Is Awesome

When I arrived, Mrs. P. greeted me and gave me a rundown of things that happened during that eternity. She said Atticus cried a river after I left that morning. She took a picture of all the children on that first day of school, so she had proof of his emotional state. After a while, he settled down, and the rest of the time ran smoothly.

Her report set the tone for the rest of the school year. Every afternoon, Mrs. P., or her assistant, Mrs. Richards, met me at the door and told me about Atticus's day. They usually had an amusing story to pass along, information on his emotional state, or they shared something he did that caught them off guard.

For instance, they were amazed at his ability to read, recognize large numbers, understand the days of the week, locate states on a map, and that he knew the names and faces of all the United States presidents. They always told me about their discoveries as if it was something I didn't know about, and they were enlightening me for the first time. I was delighted by their excitement to share their discoveries with me. In some odd way, it made me feel less lonely.

His teacher struggled with Atticus's behavior when he found something of interest. The SmartBoard and calendar were major distractions for him. Of course, both involved his two favorite things, letters and numbers, so he naturally had a hard time controlling his desire to look at them and touch them.

Atticus found a map of the United States in the classroom and began to obsess over it. Mrs. P. hid the map from him to try to keep him focused on other classroom activities, but he found it a couple of days later and became fixated once again. She finally had to hide it on the top shelf, with the map side facing the wall, so he couldn't reach it or see it again.

Mrs. P. implemented several behavioral strategies throughout the school year. All efforts to curb inappropriate behaviors eventually gave way to another. Social stories, charts, stickers, and treats were some of the popular strategies used, but none of them had a lasting effect on Atticus. According to Mrs. P., Atticus became bored with each strategy after a couple of weeks, so she was continually trying to come up with new ways to incentivize appropriate behaviors.

***

By the time December rolled around, Atticus was producing a few words that anyone could easily understand. I was surprised but grateful for the early success. We were only four months into our new journey, and the decision to enroll him in this program was already bearing fruit.

While Atticus frequently struggled to process his thoughts and produce them verbally, he never gave up. He spoke a lot of nonsense, and oftentimes became confused, which led to an inability to speak in the moment. I often wondered if he had so much information running through his brain that everything just collided into a jumbled mess, making it impossible for a coherent thought to find its way through. I pictured his mind as resembling rush-hour traffic with a multiple car pileup on the freeway—a mangled pile of progress unable to maneuver through the chaos.

His frustration escalated when words didn't come easily. I was his biggest cheerleader and greatest comforter, so when the difficult moments arose, I gently encouraged him to slow down and try to focus on what he was trying to say. Sometimes he was able to speak his thoughts, other times he wasn't.

When success came, I told him how proud I was of him. When the results didn't end as we hoped, I patted his back, told him everything would be fine, and encouraged him to never give up. I assured him that someday he would be able to convey all his thoughts with ease.

One late December morning, when I was changing his clothes, Atticus surprised me with one of his first real conversations. He said, "Mommy don't drink monkey milk." He was full of glee as he spoke the silly words.

I had no idea where his thought came from, but I found it amusing. I laughed and said, "No, mommy doesn't drink monkey milk."

"Mommy don't drink cow milk!" Atticus said.

"No, mommy doesn't drink cow milk."

He was having fun. His laughter became more pronounced when he said, "Mommy don't drink seal milk!"

"Seal milk?" I asked.

"Seal milk!" he said, squealing with delight.

"No, mommy doesn't drink seal milk."

     Hello, My Name Is Awesome

Atticus giggled and laughed over this exchange, and joy overwhelmed my soul. It was such a goofy conversation, but it was a magnificent, early sign of the progress he was experiencing.

***

Back at school, getting Atticus to use the restroom was somewhat of a challenge for all involved. Mrs. P. had a water closet in her classroom, with a child-size toilet, but Atticus refused to use it.

He was three years old, not completely potty-trained, and still wore Pull-Ups just in case there was an accident. With his refusal to use the provided restroom, Atticus had many accidents throughout the school year.

Then one day, late in the school year, Mrs. P. had an idea. She decided to take Atticus down the hall to see if he would use the office bathroom that had a regular-size toilet. Upon entering the office, Atticus saw the ceiling fan in the secretary's area and began jumping up and down, smiling, and pointing at the ceiling fan. Mrs. P. saw how happy he was and decided to strike a deal with him. If Atticus used the potty each day, she would reward him with a trip to the office to see the ceiling fan.

Atticus must have loved the arrangement because he began using the bathroom. Each time he went "pee-pee in the potty," he was escorted to the office to check out the ceiling fan in the secretary's area.

Atticus soon discovered that the principal, Mr. Brown, had a ceiling fan in his office and began visiting him as well. He loved the speed of Mr. Brown's ceiling fan. On multiple occasions he flapped his hands, jumped up and down, and enthusiastically shouted, "Mr. Brown's ceiling fan goes really, really, really fast!!" Everyone who watched got a big kick out of his love for ceiling fans, and it was one of Mrs. P's favorite stories to tell me.

One of the most memorable moments Mrs. P. relayed happened a few weeks before the school year ended. At pickup time, she looked somewhat astonished, but amused, as she retold the event of the day.

Atticus was using the restroom when he suddenly exited the door and ran through the classroom naked. Mrs. P. said Atticus was having a grand, old time. She and her assistants had to pick their jaws up off the floor before they could corral him and stop the insanity. It was hilarious and evidently one of the funniest things they experienced in quite a while.

***

The first year of preschool was eventful, and oftentimes amusing, but I never lost sight of the reason he was attending. Atticus was receiving the therapies he needed to help ensure a successful future. The evidence was stacking up—the therapies were working.

He began the school year with a severe speech delay. He entered the classroom that first day in August attempting to speak a few words that were mostly unintelligible, even to his mother's ear. By the time December rolled around, Atticus was saying words that I could easily understand. In May, at the end of the school year, he spoke in complete sentences and was able to verbalize most of his needs.

That didn't mean he was cured of all his communication issues. Atticus continued to struggle with his expressive and receptive communication. He had difficulty mentally processing and producing thoughts verbally, and he could become easily frustrated trying to do so.

He consistently mixed-up pronouns. He didn't ask questions, and he was rarely able to answer a question. He especially had difficulty with questions requiring a yes or no and even greater difficulty with why questions, which required a more articulate and detailed answer. Still, the first year of special-needs preschool produced results, and I was thrilled to have a child who was talking!

As the school year was winding down, Mrs. P. talked with me on several occasions and encouraged me to have Atticus reevaluated. She was aware of the negative results of his initial autism screening, but after spending several months with him on an almost daily basis, she believed what I had always known deep inside—Atticus was autistic. His behaviors, his sensory issues, his mannerisms, and his speech and motor delays were all signs pointing in one direction.

I questioned why I even needed a diagnosis, and she told me it wasn't as important at this stage of his life as it would be for his future educational needs. She provided the name and number of two places for me to contact to have him tested again. I didn't promise her I would, but I took the infor-

Hello, My Name Is Awesome

mation.

Mrs. P. was supposed to be his teacher the following year as well, however, a few days before school ended, she informed me that the district decided to cut the preschool program from that specific school. Atticus would be attending a new school, with a new teacher, the following year.

Tears filled our eyes as she explained the new reality. She was sad about the change but excited about the future. She said she was trusting God to make it all work.

I was less certain and a little shaken by the news. I had grown fond of Mrs. P. and her assistant, Mrs. Richards. I was looking forward to another year with them and did not want Atticus placed with another teacher.

I didn't know what was going to happen the following school year, but Mrs. P. assured me the new teacher would be more helpful and understanding than she, so I had to put the matter in the hands of God.

Even so, I had my doubts, and I didn't understand why this sudden change was taking place. Atticus had experienced so much success with this teacher; I didn't understand why God would allow this to happen. Didn't He know this was where Atticus needed to be?

But isn't that just like God?

We humans see what we think is working, so we prefer to continue traveling the same familiar road uninterrupted. After all, *it's working!* Then, something out of our control transpires and shifts our progress off course.

If you're anything like me, you begin to question "Why?" I rarely, if ever, receive an immediate answer. That's when I turn to Scripture, and I'm reminded to "Trust in the LORD with all thine heart; and lean not unto thine own understanding. In all thy ways acknowledge him, and he shall direct thy paths." Proverbs 3:5-6.

"Trust in the LORD with all thine heart…" Trusting is a complicated matter for me. A person needs to prove himself worthy of my trust, and far too often, I confuse my faith in people with my faith in God. It's just not my nature to jump headfirst into the pool of divine assurance anymore than it's my nature to trust mere mortals. I struggle with questions that have no immediate answers. I grapple for control in areas where I haven't any. I look toward the heavens and plead for intervention. At times, I feel my trust tank is running on empty when life throws me the proverbial curveball. The question "why" destroys my inner peace, and I begin to obsess. *Why would God allow this to happen?*

It's a troublesome question and one that will distort your thoughts and feelings if you don't correct your course, fix your eyes on the Almighty, and put your trust in Him. Throughout this experience, I've discovered it's not until I've traveled the reluctant road, which is often scattered with annoying potholes, menacing mountains, and threatening terrain, that I can stand back and see the glory of God in the midst of it all. As I look in the rearview mirror, I think to myself, *Why were you so afraid?* I stand in awe when I count the blessings I didn't know were in store while on the journey. It's then I realize that I need to be steadfast and remain in awe of God when faced with the unexpected. I must continue looking forward with hope and unwavering faith that He will be with me every step of this amazing life adventure.

Chapter 5
Moving Past the Diagnosis

The summer months proved more difficult than anticipated. The previous two years not only took an abrupt twist that found me struggling to come to terms with my new reality as the parent of a special-needs child, but I also watched helplessly as cancer ravaged my mother's body after a third, and final, diagnosis in 2009. The August heat ushered in the beginning of the end of summer, the loss of my mother, and Atticus's second year of preschool.

I wish I could say it was as pleasant of a beginning as the first year of school, but it wasn't. My mother passed away the day before Atticus was to turn four, and her funeral fell on the first day of school. I was unable to accompany Atticus to his new school or introduce him to his new teacher, Mrs. Downing.

No, the new school year did not begin well.

The one bright spot was that Atticus continued working with the same speech and occupational therapists as he did in his first year of preschool. I was grateful for the consistency as it meant Atticus would have professionals who were familiar to him and with his unique ways.

The first few weeks of school were tough for me. I didn't have the open communication with the new teacher like I had grown accustomed to with Mrs. P. I had no idea what was going on with Atticus during the school day. How was he behaving? How was his emotional state? Did he interact with his classmates? Were his classmates nice to him? Was he performing his work and participating in classroom activities?

I didn't have the answers to any of my questions because Atticus couldn't tell me. Yes, he could talk, but he couldn't relate events or answer questions about his day.

When I attempted interactions with his teacher on a couple of occasions, she seemed dismissive and abrupt. The situation riled me, so I decided to keep my distance and hoped things would improve as time went on. Unfortunately, or maybe fortunately as it turned out, I couldn't keep my distance for long.

A few weeks into the school year, things came to a head with Mrs. Downing and me. After a couple of short, handwritten notes traveling back and forth in Atticus's book bag, I couldn't hold back my mounting frustration any longer, so I wrote her a lengthy email.

I expressed my concerns with my son's inability to communicate with me about his day and his inability to answer questions. I addressed how I perceived her attitude and demeanor to be dismissive when I attempted to talk to her face-to-face. I proposed we might have a possible personality clash and concluded our parent/teacher relationship was not what I expected. I expressed my hope that we could resolve whatever issue there was between the two of us so nothing would interfere with Atticus getting the help he needed.

That email resulted in a meeting with Mrs. Downing and the district's preschool supervisor. From my perspective, the meeting was uncomfortable and edgy. The silence blared as we all entered the room and took our seats. One look at their sullen faces told me no one was happy to be there. My voice quivered when I spoke as I choked on my emotion.

Mrs. Downing explained that she was hurt when she read in my email that, "I don't want anything to interfere with my child getting the help he needs." She said she would never let a conflict with a parent interfere with helping a child, and I sensed she was sincere.

I expressed my desire to have questions answered and to know what was going on with Atticus during the school day. I didn't need to know every little detail, but an occasional update would be nice—especially if he was having a bad day.

Those thorny moments yielded glorious results. I believe Mrs. Downing and I both walked out of the tiny classroom that afternoon with a better understanding of each other.

Hello, My Name Is Awesome

Once our meeting ended, I was hopeful communication would improve going forward.

As months passed, Mrs. Downing and I slowly but surely developed a parent/teacher relationship that I believe rivals any in existence. Email communications occurred frequently. In the beginning, the correspondences were short and simple, but as time went on, our written conversations became lengthy, and, at times, reached far beyond the surface level happenings at school. We delved deeper into topics of Atticus's development, struggles, achievements, and shared personal happenings outside the school setting.

***

A couple of months into the school year, and with additional encouragement from Mrs. Downing, I decided to have Atticus evaluated for autism a second time. I called one of the phone numbers that Mrs. P. had provided, and thus began the second round of questionnaires, observations, developmental testing, and imaginative play.

The entire process felt like an eternity. The paperwork seemed endless. Psychologist appointments were time consuming. Questions occupied my thoughts. *Will he participate in make-believe play this time? Will he pretend the red ball is an apple? Will he sing along to the Happy Birthday song? Will his strengths outshine his weaknesses?*

The one significant difference this time around? Atticus was verbal—although he still exhibited communication deficits in several areas.

The psychologist administered the tests over a two-day period and then met with Atticus's father and me to discuss the results. As we sat on a couch in the cold, uninviting testing room, she laid out the results. Atticus met all criteria for an autism diagnosis.

My heart hurt. Even if your mind has always known something to be true, sometimes your heart isn't ready to hear it.

I don't remember his father reacting, and we never discussed it after the meeting.

I struggled to keep my emotions at bay as I listened to the psychologist explain that Atticus's severe language delay, lack of social skills, restricted interests, and repetitive behaviors all contributed to the diagnosis. She discussed things I already knew—his hand flapping, echolalia—repetitious speech where one repeats what others say, and intense interests in numbers and signs. She also discussed things I could've predicted he would do such as his repeated attempts to leave the testing area to see the numbers posted in the hallway, his inability to engage in appropriate social exchanges with her, and his failure to think imaginatively and participate in make-believe play.

I wasn't surprised because during both ADOS screenings, the examiner sat at a table with Atticus and attempted to have a pretend birthday party with him and a doll. There was a cake made of Play-Doh, with fake candles, and they were supposed to sing Happy Birthday.

On both occasions, the first ADOS screening and this latest one, Atticus had a meltdown during that part of the testing. As the examiner began to prepare for the party, he became visibly upset and tried to remove the candles from the cake. The examiner gently pushed his hand away. Once she began to sing Happy Birthday, Atticus screamed and cried uncontrollably until she stopped singing. Neither examiner was able to complete the song. He had the exact same reaction, in the same part of the test, one and a half years apart.

I watched the test, on both occasions, through an observation window. I was stunned at his behavior during the birthday portion. Atticus never seemed to have a problem at his own birthday celebrations when people sang that particular song, but he wasn't having any part of it during a pretend birthday party.

Perhaps imaginative play wasn't his strong suit.

Atticus, of course, showed strong interest in academics, but the psychologist warned of future educational needs when the ability to comprehend reading materials becomes a necessity and other subjects become more abstract and difficult to understand. She encouraged that these areas are not overlooked and should be closely monitored by his educational team.

Mrs. Downing was happy Atticus received the diagnosis. She believed it would be beneficial for his academic success. She told me on many occasions that in her twenty years of teaching she had never met a child quite like Atticus. He constantly said and did things that blew her away, and she told me how brilliant she believed him to be; however, she also knew his weaknesses needed to be addressed in an official capacity, or he could end up falling through the educational cracks, labeled with behavioral issues, and deemed a troubled child.

That wasn't going to happen on our watch.

***

Once we all settled into the new school year and the testing was complete, it didn't take Mrs. Downing long to realize her typical system to encourage good behavior didn't work for Atticus, but she soon discovered one that did.

Mrs. Downing recognized how much Atticus loved to write, so she decorated the cover of a three-ring binder and labeled it *Atticus's Journal*. He also loved to play word games on the computer. Mrs. Downing took a picture of the computer and a picture of the journal. She then cut each picture into four pieces, placed Velcro on the back, and pieced the pictures together on two separate pieces of card stock. At the beginning of each school day, she presented Atticus with a choice of which item he wanted to earn that day—the computer or the writing journal. If he behaved inappropriately throughout the day, he received one verbal warning. If he continued with the behavior, one picture was removed. If all four pictures were removed before the end of the day, he didn't receive a reward.

Atticus loved the computer and journal so much that this system worked like a charm, and Mrs. Downing never had to try a different strategy. It worked so well, in fact, that I implemented the system in our home with great success as well.

Atticus matured so much during his first year with Mrs. Downing, and over the summer, that during his second year with her, he no longer needed his own reward system and was able to participate in the same system as his classmates—sweet success!

***

Atticus's two years with Mrs. Downing provided many learning experiences, some trials, a few distractions, and a couple of frightening situations for him.

Victoria Layne

Such was the case with the unexpected fire drill.

At the beginning of each school year, I inform Atticus's new teachers about his fear of fire alarms, so they can prepare him in advance when they know a drill is going to take place. In this case, none of the teachers had any idea the surprise fire drill was going to happen. As the class was going about their day, the alarm blared in the classroom, and Atticus immediately covered his ears and cried. The noise terrified and overwhelmed him.

Mrs. Downing's assistant took Atticus's hand to comfort him, and he held on tightly. He was able to calm himself a bit once they reached their outdoor destination, but when all was clear and they reentered the classroom, Atticus was crying again.

Mrs. Downing asked him what was wrong, and he responded through his tears, "Mom parks in a no-parking fire lane." Of course, I don't park in a fire lane, but that was the only way Atticus could answer Mrs. Downing's question, and she understood that he was expressing his distress and turmoil over the fire alarm.

One of the most mysterious and strangest events took place after Christmas break. Atticus couldn't answer questions in a fully functional manner yet, so it took a while to unravel this conundrum.

Atticus seemed excited as he made his way back to school that January, but once he arrived inside the building, he began crying profusely. He then told Mrs. Downing he didn't want to go into her classroom, but he wanted to go to the other preschool room instead. She told him that wasn't an option, so he reluctantly walked into his normal classroom.

He continued crying once school was underway.

When circle time rolled around, his crying turned to screaming, and Atticus told Mrs. Downing he was scared. Later that day, Mrs. Downing observed him staring into space, then bursting into tears again without warning. She was unable to identify the problem.

That evening, like most evenings, I asked Atticus a couple of questions about his day. By this time, he was able to answer some yes and no questions, but he struggled to answer open-ended questions. I usually didn't receive any type of answer from him, and on the rare occasion he attempted to answer, his words seldom made sense. I continued to ask in the hope that someday

Hello, My Name Is Awesome

he could answer and that his answers would be flawless and easy to understand. Occasionally, I could glean something about his day if I made statements rather than asked questions. So, I would make comments such as, "School was fun today," or "Let's talk about your day!" He either responded to my prompting, or he wouldn't.

On this particular evening, he told me, "I am upset at school." This shocked me, as everything seemed fine throughout the evening. What could he possibly be upset about? I told him that if he tells me what is wrong, I will fix it.

His pouty lips said, "I want mommy to fix it."

I replied again, "You need to tell me what is wrong, so I can fix it."

Atticus said, "There's a big ocean."

What? A big ocean? That's all he's giving me? What am I supposed to do with that?

I repeated, "Tell me what's wrong so I can fix it."

He wailed, "There's lots and lots of countries!"

Big ocean? Lots of countries? I had no idea why he was so upset, but he was literally listing things on a map, so I asked him if there was a map in Mrs. Downing's classroom. Without hesitation, he cried, "Yes!"

I was at a loss. He was upset, so I comforted him, but I had no clue why he was distressed over a map. Atticus has loved maps for as far back as I can remember, so I couldn't figure out why he would be upset unless he wasn't allowed access to the map.

Once Atticus calmed down, he was able to go to sleep. I then checked my email and found a note from Mrs. Downing telling me about his odd day.

I responded to her email and let her know about the conversation Atticus and I had about the ocean, the countries, and his emotional state. She confirmed she had a large world map on the classroom wall and that Atticus chose to sit beside the map during circle time all year without any problems until that day.

Neither one of us had any idea what was going on with him, but the next day at school, he displayed obvious anxiety once again. He told Mrs. Downing he would stay with her during circle time. He was visibly shaking with fear as he stood beside her. She tried to comfort him and give him positive feedback, but nothing worked.

On the third day, his fear was present once again. Mrs. Downing sat him on her lap and asked him why he was afraid. He told her he was afraid of the map. She immediately removed the map from the wall, but Atticus refused to believe it was gone. He refused to look in that direction. After some cajoling, he finally peeked at the spot where the map used to be, discovered it was gone, and his fear left him—never to return.

Mrs. Downing and I were bewildered. Neither of us understood why he suddenly developed a fear of that map, nor was he able to tell us.

Months later, while lying on the couch at home, Atticus asked me where his interactive Cars (the movie) map was. It was then that I remembered his aunt bought him the interactive toy, which took him around the world with Lightening McQueen, for Christmas. After he played with the map for a few days, he wanted me to put it away. I thought it strange at the time, but I didn't attempt to question him. I simply put the map in a cabinet and didn't give it a second thought.

Now, months later, he was asking about the map. I told him it's in the cabinet and asked him if he wanted to play with it. He answered, "No," while appearing to become a bit upset.

After inquiring further about his emotional state and trying to figure out why he didn't want the map, he finally said, "The Leaning Tower of Pisa."

Once again, his words confused me. *What about the Leaning Tower of Pisa?* The interactive map took him to Italy and talked about the tower, but so what? Then it hit me. "Do you think the tower is going to fall and hurt you?"

"Yes," he replied.

Everything began to make sense. "Is that why you were afraid of the map in Mrs. Downing's classroom?" I asked.

"Yes," he said.

Finally, I solved the mystery. When the interactive map talked about the Leaning Tower of Pisa, Atticus literally thought the leaning tower was going to fall on him. No wonder the poor child wanted the toy out of his sight and was terrified of the world map in Mrs. Downing's class!

Atticus and I discussed the matter for quite a while, and he somehow

Hello, My Name Is Awesome

rationalized and believed me when I told him the tower wasn't anywhere near the maps. The tower was in Italy, which was thousands of miles away from us, and it's only leaning, not falling on anyone. We looked at pictures of the tower on the Internet and saw that it was still standing.

After several minutes, I talked him into looking at the interactive map again. I held his hand as we crept to the cabinet. I continued to reassure him that the tower wouldn't fall, and he would be completely safe. I calmly opened the door and pulled out the map. I held it while Atticus stared at it. I pushed a few buttons to show him nothing bad was going to happen. After a few moments, he realized he was safe, took the map, and played with it as though nothing had ever happened.

Chapter 6
Triumphs

Atticus suffered occasional meltdowns throughout the school year, but the reasons for his emotional outbursts usually remained a mystery. He had great difficulty explaining why he felt a certain way. If he gave any answer at all, his reply was that he was, "Upset," or "Tired," but no details accompanied those words.

As part of the daily routine, the class would dance and sing during circle time. A few months into the school year, Mrs. Downing and her entire class experienced the wrath of Atticus when a song was selected that he did not want to hear.

His verbal protest escalated into endless screams—screams that wouldn't stop even after he was placed in timeout or when he lost all the pictures for his reward that day. He continued to scream so loudly, and so long, that the principal came into the classroom to make sure everything was all right. Mrs. Downing assured the principal that everything was fine, and the class was ignoring Atticus and his behavior.

I have been dealing with this problem since he began talking. If a song came on the radio that he didn't want to hear, or if I decided to sing while driving or doing household chores, he would demand I "Stop singing," or "Turn off the radio." If I refused, he would cry, he would scream, he would yell at me to turn off the music. This behavior became louder and more obnoxious until I turned off the music or the song was over. He turned perfectly joyful moments into unexplained turmoil and caused me to feel hopeless at times.

It's impossible to maintain a positive attitude while this behavior is happening, so I usually ended up screaming at him to stop his screaming,

Hello, My Name Is Awesome

and then I turned the music up, which only intensified his meltdown. He would have rather died screaming for the song to stop than accept that it will continue. The results were truly some of the ugliest moments between the two of us.

On Atticus's second go-round with Mrs. Downing, she was better equipped to handle the song situation. When his screaming and crying began, she told him he had two options—earmuffs or headphones.

She presented both to Atticus and told him he could put the earmuffs or headphones over his ears if he didn't want to listen to everyone sing, but he must participate in song time. He chose the earmuffs, and it worked! She continued to allow him to choose between the two items throughout the school year.

I'm still not sure what triggers this reaction with certain songs.

During this period, I thought it best to inform Mrs. Downing about Atticus's meltdowns during the ADOS screening when the examiner attempted to sing Happy Birthday.

I didn't know it at the time, but every year she has a birthday party for each student. Since Atticus's birthday usually falls a couple of days before the school year begins, Mrs. Downing planned a fake fifth birthday celebration for him near the end of the school year.

I reminded her of the issue with the Happy Birthday song, and she was prepared. Atticus wore the fluffy, pink earmuffs while his class sang Happy Birthday, and he didn't shed a single tear.

***

Despite occasional meltdowns and communication issues, Atticus's two years with Mrs. Downing saw huge progress and great success. He was becoming more and more verbal and eager to speak to the world.

He didn't have any problems approaching complete strangers to ask them a question about their age or some other topic that may have interested him in the moment. He acted on impulse regularly and didn't seem to have any inhibitions, which was and still is a little unnerving for me.

While the professionals in his school continued to work with him on his social, emotional, and sensory needs, I spent many days working with him on manners and patience in real-life situations such as grocery shopping, eating in restaurants, or participating in a public event. I felt it necessary to immerse him into as many situations as I could possibly afford and could commit the time.

He attended his first play at age four. I wasn't sure how he would handle the environment of a theater, but I was willing to find out. *If You Give a Mouse a Cookie* was one of his favorite books, so the live stage production seemed like the logical choice to introduce him to the theater.

The play was forty minutes long, and twenty minutes into the performance, Atticus announced, "I'm done."

The theater was small and quite intimate, making the audience feel as though they were in the middle of the action on stage. I am certain the emotions coming from the actors, along with the loud sound effects and music bursting out of the speakers, was a bit overwhelming for him.

I was able to keep him in the room for another five minutes before he told me he had to use the restroom. We left the theater, and, of course, he didn't have to use the restroom. He just didn't want to be in the theater any longer.

I allowed him a few minutes to walk around and release some pent-up energy. He eventually agreed to go back inside to watch the end of the play. Afterward, he happily met with the "mouse" and had his picture taken with her.

He made it through the entire experience without crying or screaming. Yes, there came a point when he required a break, but he was able to verbalize his need. Once we met his need, we completed the task. I was super proud of him.

I told Mrs. Downing about our outing, and she was thrilled. She encouraged me to continue exposing him to public events such as this. She expressed her desire that all parents would be as bold in exposing their children to these types of situations.

Many parents of autistic children shy away from public events for fear of stares or rude comments from strangers who have no clue about their situation. I try not to give that any thought. I've been determined from the beginning that the only way Atticus was going to learn how to behave ap-

Hello, My Name Is Awesome

propriately in public situations was to expose him as often as possible and verbally correct his behavior as necessary—even if it meant I repeat myself thirty times an hour.

I'm confident I've had my share of stares and strangers making judgmental comments to each other about my parenting or my child's behavior, but I've never noticed. I've always dealt with Atticus directly and ignored the world around us.

I'm a disciplinarian by nature, so I have little patience for over-the-top behavior—especially in a public setting. If a situation becomes too chaotic, I'm quick to remove both of us from the room out of respect for others, and let Atticus know his behavior is unacceptable.

This wasn't and still isn't an easy task. Once he and I reach a certain point, emotions run high for both of us, and the ugliness can last quite a while. As hard as it is on me mentally and emotionally, I refuse to give in to certain behaviors, and I believe they need to be dealt with in the moment— even if the moment turns into an hour or two.

***

The greatest triumph from his preschool years came when Atticus was four years and four months old. He was on Christmas break from school when a prayer that I had prayed countless times was answered from out of the blue. On December 22, 2011, Atticus asked his first question!

"What is it made of?" he asked, holding a candy cane.

I was overwhelmed with joy!

But God didn't stop there. A few minutes later, He followed that miracle with yet another one. Atticus was looking at a silver dollar, something he had done many times in his short life, only this time he showed me the coin and asked, "Who is on it?"

Yes, my God is still in the miracle business.

Up to that point, I had mentioned to a couple of people that Atticus never asked questions. Each person had the same response— "You're lucky."

I'm aware they didn't realize how insensitive they were being with their remarks. They never had a child who struggled to communicate. They never spent countless hours urging their child to produce a single syllable. They never experienced silence where there should have been sound. All they had to draw on was their own experience, and their experience was the exact opposite of mine.

They were blessed with neurotypical children who asked numerous questions from an early age. There was no way for these parents to understand the pain associated with a child who didn't speak or inquire about life, so how were they to understand what a gut-wrenching blow the words, "You're lucky," were to me. My response to them was, "You wouldn't think you were lucky if it was your child."

But now, my Atticus, who God often continues to work miracles through, was asking questions. A couple of days later, on Christmas Eve, he asked two more questions, and the frequency continued to increase going forward.

The following summer, at the age of four years and ten months, another prayer was answered when Atticus was able to pedal and ride a bike for the first time—with training wheels, of course.

He often struggled with riding a tricycle and never mastered the pedaling. At the age of three, I bought him a bike because a therapist told me it would be easier to pedal. He didn't have any luck with that either. The only way that bike was moving was if I pushed it.

Now, a year later, and just two months shy of my son's fifth birthday, he pedaled the bike on his own for the first time. My enthusiasm for his progress was over the rainbow.

***

Atticus flourished in the preschool setting, and his progress was astonishing. But he continued to struggle with the core issues of communication, sensory overload, social behaviors, and the rare emotional outburst.

Along with his ability to ask questions, his social interactions increased. He was quick to initiate conversation with adults and was happy to talk with them endlessly—as long as the topic remained on his subject of choice. He greeted adults and children alike. He didn't, however, understand social cues, often droning on endlessly about the same topic and invading an individual's personal space.

He began to share his thoughts and ideas in the classroom setting when urged to participate in conversation, and he could participate in circle time and all classroom activities without a one-on-one aide. Academically, he shined, but he continued to show weakness in the areas of comprehension and inference.

Atticus saw a little improvement with his fine motor skills but continued to struggle with sensory, self-regulation, and motor planning. Despite his continued struggles, I was constantly amazed with his progress and development over the course of his two years with Mrs. Downing.

A few weeks prior to the end of his preschool run, Mrs. Downing sent me an email. She wanted me to know how adored Atticus was by all the professionals who had worked with him the previous three years, and how much he would be missed by all of them. She specifically wanted to tell me that one of them told her, "You know, there are some children who touch your heart in ways that you can't explain, and Atticus is one of them."

I cried as I read her words. The fact that my sweet, unique boy had such a positive and loving impact on others moved me. He was surely turning into a force of good and a blessing to many.

As our time with Mrs. Downing wound down, I realized how much of our personal life I had shared with her in the past twenty-four months. Despite our bumpy beginning, it wasn't long before I perceived her to be someone who knew and understood Atticus almost as well as I did, and she loved him dearly. I was cognizant that I no longer had my mother to share Atticus with, and Mrs. Downing had become a substitute of sorts.

She was a safe place for me to discuss the amazing things Atticus randomly surprised me with. I knew I wouldn't be judged as braggadocios because she understood who he was and the things he was capable of doing. I knew that she was always proud of him. She was someone with whom I could share the joy, frustration, and pure fascination that Atticus brought to me daily. She appreciated him, knew his abilities, and saw his potential.

I grew attached to Mrs. Downing over the course of Atticus's two years with her. I was thankful that God once again had placed the perfect person in our lives to help guide us through that time.

While I was more than four years into this journey, I still had much to learn. Mrs. Downing, with twenty years of special-needs experience, was a wealth of knowledge, and I sought her help on a multitude of issues and situations. I honestly didn't know how I was going to handle moving forward with Atticus's academic life without her, but the time had come, and we were forced to move on.

Mrs. Downing and I had several discussions prior to Atticus's transition to kindergarten. She provided her professional and personal opinions on the educational course we should chart in the future.

She stressed repeatedly that I shouldn't allow Atticus to get lost in the system, and she presented a list of several options I had to choose from to begin his academic life. I eagerly absorbed all the information and advice she provided. In much the same way Atticus's former speech therapist had encouraged me to always advocate for him, Mrs. Downing urged me to carefully consider my options and do what I believed was best for him educationally.

I was grateful that God gave Mrs. Downing and I the ability to look beyond our rocky beginning and develop a relationship that I'm confident was largely responsible for the tremendous growth Atticus experienced during those two years. I believe our partnership contributes to his academic success to this day. The foundation we built together has been priceless. Never underestimate the power of two strong women working together toward a common goal—or the power of God to provide.

I'm reminded of the often-used Scripture passage that declares, "And we know that all things work together for the good to them that love God, to them who are the called according to his purpose" Romans 8:28.

When I first encountered Mrs. Downing, I had little faith that anything good would come out of our affiliation, but God had other plans. He knew exactly where Atticus needed to be, and He knew exactly who Atticus needed to be with. God stood with Atticus and never left his side. As our initial icy association evolved into an active and respectful partnership, I watched my child's communication increase as his gentle spirit emerged to bless the lives of others. Whether they knew it or not, God's love touched their lives in the moments of joy they experienced with this exceptional boy.

In the process, my faith continued to strengthen. I rejoiced that God

Hello, My Name Is Awesome

could indeed "make all things work for the good." I believed, beyond the shadow of a doubt, that He would always take care of Atticus and had tremendous plans for his future.

Chapter 7
A School that Welcomes God

Preparing to move forward was a tiresome, anxiety-inducing task. What school should he attend? What type of educational environment was best suited for him? Public? Christian? Catholic? Montessori? What school had a program that was best equipped to help children like Atticus succeed? Would I make the correct decision?

I visited several schools in an attempt to answer these questions. Each visit resulted in more questions. Who were these strangers? Could I trust them? Did they have my child's best interest at heart? The process of the unknown overwhelmed me.

After much angst, consideration, reconsideration, and prayer, I decided to have Atticus spend his kindergarten year attending a school that specializes in autism. I based my decision on several factors, including a parent referral, interviews with the administration, and a tour of the school.

While the school's campus was far from impressive, the program resonated with me, and I thought I was making a wise decision, even if I was hesitant about sending him to a school whose main focus was autistic children.

From the moment I suspected that Atticus was autistic, I was adamant that he wouldn't be defined by a label. I strived to make his life and surroundings as normal as possible. That included making sure any activities, such as gymnastic classes or tennis lessons, were not special-needs based but typical everyday events with typical everyday children. I wouldn't even discuss autism in his presence because I didn't want this brilliant child of mine to use his diagnosis as an excuse for not trying his best or tackling challenging situations. I knew he faced various struggles, both physically and mentally, but giving up was not an option. So the decision to send him to a school geared toward autism was difficult.

One factor that weighed heavily was the assurance that each classroom would have a 4:1 student/teacher ratio. I relished the idea that Atticus would be in a small-group learning environment where he would be free to perform at his own level and progress at his own pace. I feared that his strong academic abilities would be overlooked instead of supported and encouraged in a large classroom setting, so the ratio appealed to me.

During my initial interview with the school, I stressed how important it was to me that Atticus would have typical developing children in his classroom. I received assurances that peer models were part of the program, but on the first day of kindergarten, we arrived in his classroom to discover there wasn't a peer model to be found—and there wouldn't be. This was a huge problem as far as I was concerned and the first red flag of many. Sadly, it was evident from the first day of school that I had made the wrong choice.

The parent who provided the referral pulled her child out of the school after the first couple of weeks and decided to homeschool. She said the school had changed so much over the summer that it didn't even seem like the same place her child attended the previous year.

Because I had a great feeling about the new, first-year teacher in Atticus's classroom, I decided to allow him to complete the year, but it wasn't easy. While his classroom had mostly high-functioning children, he was exposed to severe behavioral problems and violence from other children, especially when his class joined others at recess.

The number of children in Atticus's class continued to increase as the school year marched on, while the number of teachers remained the same— one. So much for the 4:1 ratio. I spent a generous amount of time expressing my displeasure to the administrator over the lack of teacher support in Atticus's classroom.

There were a few bright spots, however. Atticus brought to the school a joyful, kind, and loving spirit. He interacted with many of the adults throughout the school, and I was often told how he brightened their days.

On one occasion, his teacher shared with me that other personnel in the building would come to see Atticus when they were having a rough day. They told her that he made people happy, and I've found that to be true.

Adults he interacts with—whether we're at church, a grocery store, a restaurant, or wherever Atticus decides to spread his special brand of happiness, have often told me the same thing. I was thankful he touched the staff in such a loving and beautiful way.

As we were leaving the school one afternoon, he stopped to talk with one of the teachers. I overheard her ask him, "Do you *ever* have a bad day? I bet you never have a bad day!" He told her he didn't, but I knew otherwise.

I was struck with her analysis that Atticus "never" had a bad day. The outside world looks at Atticus, and they see a joyful, calming personality. His ready smile and accepting disposition welcomes others and warms their hearts. His delightful expression and uninhibited desire to connect with others is unstoppable. I've watched as he approaches people that most of us overlook. I've witnessed moments such as the time he intentionally walked over to the hunchbacked, seventy-year-old supermarket worker and gifted her with a simple wave, a warm smile, and a cheerful, "Hello!"

I observed as she weakly looked up from the cookies she placed on the table, realized he was talking to her, and I saw a bright smile transform her expression as she said, "Hello," in return. Her tragic demeanor suddenly grew strong and happy, as if she was standing straight again for the first time in years.

When I see God working through Atticus in those moments, I wish I could be that kind of vessel—the type of person who brightens your day. The type of person who touches your heart. The type of person who outsiders think never has a bad day.

The other bright spot at school was his teacher. She was phenomenal in the sense that she was patient, kind, and Atticus loved her. She realized his academic strengths immediately and did her best to work with him at his advanced level and challenge him as often as possible. This was a difficult task for months, however, because the classroom didn't have the student/teacher ratio that had been promised. When I complained, the administrator repeatedly told me they couldn't find anyone who wanted a part-time job to fill the position. My thought was, *That's fine, but you should have limited the classroom size to four children if that was the case.*

I eventually became so disgusted with the situation that I requested

Hello, My Name Is Awesome

the necessary information regarding the position and asked if I could post the job description on my Facebook page. At that point, God provided once again, and the school hired someone from my church for the assistant's position.

***

One running theme throughout the school year was the subject of God. Atticus loved to talk about God and often spoke boldly about our Creator.

About halfway through the school year, he was discussing God in his classroom when his teacher told him he wasn't allowed to talk about that subject in school. This upset Atticus greatly and affected him the remainder of the school year.

That evening, he told me that his teacher said he couldn't talk about God and that makes him very sad. I explained to him that his teacher was wrong, and she should not have told him that.

The following day, I discussed the situation with her. I explained that while she may be prohibited from teaching religion inside the classroom, Atticus has every right to speak about God at home, at school, or anywhere else he desires. Atticus was aware of our discussion. He was told he could talk about God, but he wouldn't talk about the subject at school from that point forward.

Throughout the remainder of the school year, this weighed heavily on his heart. In our private moments together, he often repeated, "I'm not allowed to talk about God at school," and he refused to believe otherwise. On several occasions, he expressed a desire to attend a school where he was free to talk about God and worship our Savior as often as he wanted. Unfortunately, there wasn't anything I could do at that point to make his wishes a reality.

***

At the beginning of his kindergarten year, I decided that Atticus wouldn't return to that school for first grade. By the end of the year, it was clear I had made the right decision. Mercifully, the year ended without any major physical or emotional trauma.

The news that Atticus was leaving the school didn't sit well with a couple of parents. They were sad to hear that he was departing because they enjoyed his presence in the classroom and were planning for their children to return. I explained that I had to do what was best for my child and this school didn't meet his needs.

A few months prior to the school year ending, I began the arduous task of finding a fresh, new environment suited to Atticus's educational needs. The problem was, my convenient choices were limited, and none of them looked promising.

I often considered homeschooling him, but since I had to work outside the home, I knew this would be impossible.

Although Atticus attended public schools for three years of special-needs preschool, I was not thrilled with the idea of sending him to a public school for his elementary years and beyond. He would be mainstreamed into a regular classroom, but a parent told me that all children with IEP's were lumped together in one room, and I knew that wouldn't benefit Atticus in the least.

Even if that rumor wasn't true, I didn't get the feeling that public schools were right for him. Large classrooms; noisy, crowded hallways, playgrounds, and cafeterias; and the inability to speak up for himself would either doom him to a life of invisibility or create problematic behaviors that could threaten his ability to learn and coexist in that environment.

I interviewed with a private Christian school close to home, but after meeting with the principal and supplying her with a mountain of information concerning Atticus, I didn't have a good feeling. As expected, the school didn't have an intervention program in place, and at that point no one was sure how Atticus would function inside a classroom without specialized teachers and therapists involved. The principal thanked me for meeting with her and for my honesty regarding Atticus's strengths and weaknesses. She seemed overwhelmed by the verbal information I provided, but she wanted to wait until she read his IEP before making a formal decision.

A few days later, she contacted me and said she didn't think the school was equipped with the staff necessary to help Atticus be successful. I was

Hello, My Name Is Awesome

disappointed, but not surprised. I sensed she may have felt that way when we first spoke. I was oddly at peace with her decision.

I didn't panic or let the setback deter me. I took a deep breath and remained faithful that God would eventually lead me to where Atticus could learn. Even in the stormiest of times, the Lord always watched over Atticus.

Because of my son's autism diagnosis, he was eligible to receive a scholarship for educational needs. Since the non-scholarship option I was hoping for didn't pan out, I perused the scholarship website hoping for a comparable alternative. I found a list of educational providers and searched each provider's website. I read various reviews and discovered that all the institutions appeared to focus solely on autism, or autism and other developmental needs. I simply couldn't go down that road again. Moreover, Atticus desperately wanted to attend a school where he could speak freely about God. I began to feel slightly discouraged—then, a name caught my eye.

A single, private Christian school was listed as a provider. I couldn't believe it. I researched the school online and found many glowing reviews. The location was a good distance from our home though. *I don't want to make that long drive every day—twice a day.* But something told me to call and tour the school anyway.

Upon arrival, the friendly receptionist greeted me then informed the principal I had arrived for our meeting. The principal provided a tour of the campus and supplied information about the school's policies, curriculum, intervention program, and student body.

This was a typical K-6 Christian school, which happened to include a special-needs program that allows high-functioning children like Atticus the chance to attend a Christ-centered school and to be mainstreamed in the classroom with typically developing peers.

The intervention program was already established, and obviously near and dear to the principal's heart. The school was equipped to serve kids like Atticus with a speech therapist and intervention specialists who were all prepared to assist children throughout their time at the school.

They also offered an enrichment program, violin, band, choir, Spanish, art, gym, technology classes, musical theater, and after-school programs. It sounded too good to be true, but it was.

After the tour, the principal and I went back to her office and spent another hour discussing the school, Atticus, and my hopes for his future. Before I left our meeting, I knew this was where Atticus belonged and thanked God for guiding me to this place and coming through for Atticus again. I no longer cared about the distance from our home.

After our meeting, Atticus participated in a shadow day with the kindergarten class. The principal and staff had to observe his behavior and make sure he was capable of functioning in a neurotypical classroom setting. Shadow day was a success, and I received glowing reviews from both the teacher and Atticus.

With grateful hearts and a renewed hope for his future, Atticus was accepted as a student, and he started his first-grade year in a new and permanent school. While standing in the prayer circle the morning of the first day of school, I was overwhelmed with God's love and devotion to my child. I wept as the principal welcomed the students and parents back for the new year and her audible prayer rose to heaven.

It didn't take long for Atticus to feel safe and happy inside the school walls. He cherished going to chapel every Wednesday with his classmates. Although he continued to struggle with meltdowns over people singing certain songs in certain situations, he loved gospel music and adored singing songs of worship and praise to our Savior. He would tell anyone who listened that he used to go to a school where he wasn't allowed to talk about God, but now he could talk about God whenever he wanted. He was proud of that truth. Yes, Atticus was finally where he belonged, and his spirit soared.

He will continue to attend this school until he graduates from the highest grade offered. Mainstreamed with typical developing peers in a Christ-centered educational environment, he is thriving. His grades have been exemplary—all As with a couple of stray Bs through the years. He has won district spelling bees for his given grade levels, participated in math competitions and after-school clubs, and has learned to communicate about his day as he continues to figure out how to express himself and share information when he gets home in the evenings. I no longer need to worry if something happens to him when he is away from home. Through the grace of God, my child is now able to tell me.

     Hello, My Name Is Awesome

He has also participated in two school musicals. Atticus enjoys acting and singing and has performed in church programs since he was four years old, so when he was eligible to audition for a musical in third grade, he jumped at the chance. He played Bundles the laundry man and Drake the butler in *Annie Jr.* He shined in both roles. In fourth grade, he snagged the part of Chef Louis in the Disney classic *The Little Mermaid Jr.* He worked tirelessly to learn a French accent and practice the choreography, which does not come easily to him. He stole the show with his comedic portrayal of the bombastic chef. Parents and teachers alike couldn't stop telling me how impressed they were with his performance.

Atticus continues to receive speech and occupational therapy on a weekly basis. He struggles in many areas—mentally processing information, social interactions, assertiveness—but he enjoys going to school each day, being with his classmates, and interacting with the faculty and staff. Caring professionals surround him, and for the most part, his classmates are generous and kind. But as he ages, he is becoming aware of how different he is from his peers and realizing that not everyone is truly his friend.

There have been challenges along the way, but the positive aspects far outweigh the negative, and I'm confident Atticus is where God wants him to be.

In his second-grade year, his classmate Aylah was the first child to ask Atticus on a play date. He was so excited to come home and give me the map to her house that she drew for him. He told me about the time they spent together at recess planning their day together. I contacted Aylah's mom and discovered that this was just as big of a surprise to her as it was to me, but we scheduled a time for all of us to meet at the park so the two of them could play.

Atticus had a wonderful time with Aylah that bright, beautiful Saturday morning. They chased each other around the playground, played hide-and-seek, climbed ropes, and ran on the bridge. As I stood watching them, I choked back tears, thinking that this is what moms of typical kids must feel like. Or maybe not. Maybe they could never understand the significance of that moment for me.

My son had a friend who wanted to spend time with him, and it touched me in a way I can't adequately explain. That little girl will always hold a special place in my heart for the kindness she showed Atticus, not only by inviting him on a play date, but the way I have seen her go out of her way to speak to him and show him kindness since. She is a shining example of God's abundant generosity in Atticus's life.

The psalmist proclaimed, "Thou hast caused men to ride over our head; we went through fire and through water; but thou broughtest us out into a wealthy place" Psalm 66:12. This powerful passage speaks of turmoil and adversity, but it also speaks of God's goodness. I can relate.

I remember when Atticus first received his diagnosis. I had long known that he was autistic, but I never wanted an official diagnosis. I suppose I was trying to protect my heart. Perhaps autism didn't exist if there wasn't a diagnosis attached. Nevertheless, there I found myself, sitting in the cold, lonely testing room, listening to the psychologist reveal her findings. I wasn't the same after that.

I stewed for days. Unsure of how I should feel but knowing that I didn't like the truth I had been presented. I wanted to cry. I wanted to scream. *Why was this happening? Why is life so unfair?*

At first, I wouldn't discuss Atticus's diagnosis with anyone except the professionals involved. I didn't want him to go through life with this label. I eventually decided that I needed to talk to someone, so I scheduled a meeting with Pastor Dan. We met in his office on a cold, cloudy February morning. I was heartbroken as I spoke the words for the first time aloud, "Atticus is autistic." I crumbled midway through and sobbed as I finished my short sentence.

I struggled to breathe as I tried in vain to explain why this diagnosis was so upsetting to me. *Why is this so hard? Why do I feel so sad? Other parents have it worse than me. My child has many problems, but at least he can talk!*

Dan remained calm. He handed me a box of tissues as I attempted to apologize for my emotional outburst. He told me not to apologize. He told me it was okay to cry. As I tried to collect myself and regain control, I thought, *He must think I'm crazy.*

Dan filled my sudden silence with words of encouragement. He quoted a few Scriptures and spoke a couple clichés. We conversed for well over

Hello, My Name Is Awesome

an hour, but I couldn't seem to open my mouth without crying. Eventually, he made an analogy that struck a chord within me. He said he was reminded of Simon. Not Simon Peter, but Simon of Cyrene—the man who bore Jesus' cross.

Simon didn't just happen to be traveling the route that led him to an encounter with a beaten and exhausted Jesus that day. The encounter was preordained. Simon was positioned in that place, at that time, to bear the cross of a man who would bear the sins of the world. Dan said he didn't know what plans God had for Atticus's future, but he knew that Atticus was specifically born to me—in this place—at this time. It was now my job to help him grow and become the person that God predestined him to be. I found comfort in his words and determined, once again, that I would support my child, advocate for him, and do whatever it took to help him be successful in life.

Yes, I have travelled "through the fire and through the water," and I have glimpsed the "wealthy place." God's love is abundant and unquestioned when I reflect on the road that Atticus and I have traveled together. The desolate, barren desert when my child couldn't speak a word. The physical struggles, the neurological challenges, the dreaded diagnosis. Yet, we have seen success, and I almost feel embarrassed with riches. I know a lot of parents don't witness the same progress that I have. However, I'm not embarrassed. I'm thankful. And I can't wait to see what God has in store for his future.

Chapter 8
Growing Pains

Every child will experience growing pains. Whether those pains are physical, emotional, or mental, anyone who has survived to adulthood has suffered many in their younger years.

The neurotypical child faces many challenges, but an autistic child, by default, will struggle more with communication, emotional issues, social connections, self-care, and multiple delays. And while life can be demanding and exhausting for all of us, I believe we can find a mix of humor, inspiration, and learning in what may seem like meaningless moments at the time.

I tried to never overlook the "meaningless moments" with Atticus. I felt so blessed to have a child who could *finally* talk that each moment we shared felt like a miracle to me. Happy, sad, joyful, grumpy, I embraced them all—even when I was pushed to the brink. So blessed am I, that most of our moments have brought more laughter than tears.

Nevertheless, I must share both the good and bad. The following moments delivered comical, thought provoking, and heart-wrenching moments. I hope when he is grown, he can look back on this stage of his life as fondly as I.

***

Journal Entry
December 2010
3 Years 4 Months Old

Children on the autism spectrum can be a nightmare to potty train. Some, unfortunately, never become proficient in this department, while others will flourish even if it takes a little extra time than typical-developing children.

Hello, My Name Is Awesome

Atticus finally learned to tell me when he has to pee. He has known the sign for *potty* for over a year now, but this summer, he began using the gesture to let me know he has to go. After almost two years of speech therapy, he recently began using some words in a coherent fashion and now verbally tells me.

Of course, we still have moments when he doesn't alert me, but for the most part, that area of concern is going pretty well during his waking hours. Going poopy in the potty, however, is not going quite as well.

I've never been a mother who bribes her child to do something, but like many parents, I've been pushed to the brink of insanity when it comes to potty training, and I'll try almost anything to make dirty underwear a thing of the past.

I recently discovered that Atticus loves ice cream. Occasionally, as a special treat, I'll buy non-dairy ice cream for his enjoyment. It didn't take me long to realize ice cream is his favorite treat, so I resorted to offering him a taste of the frozen treat if he will start pooping in the potty. This brilliant idea has yet to show any sign of success.

This evening, I was home alone while Atticus and his dad were enjoying a boy's night out. Their time together usually consists of trips to home improvement stores and dinner at the Cracker Barrel. This is a pleasant opportunity because it affords me the luxury of alone time. It's a time when I can take a break from my role as a mother and focus on myself; a time when I can reflect on my life and situation; a time when I can do whatever I please because it's my time to enjoy, and I take advantage of it. Tonight, I decided to indulge myself with an oversized bowl of chocolate chip ice cream.

I had just filled my bowl, sat down on the living room couch, and took three bites of ice cream when Atticus and his dad walked through the front door. I had no time to react. Atticus immediately saw that I had ice cream. In a panic, I exclaimed, "Mommy pooped in the potty, so she gets ice cream!"

He ran over to me and my bowl full of ice cream. As I lifted the spoon to take a bite, his mouth followed the ice cream. He chomped air as I pulled the spoon away and said, "No! You don't poop in the potty—you don't get ice cream."

Atticus's dad interjected, "Someone pooped in his underwear this evening."

Atticus repeated, "Pooped in underwear."

I looked at Atticus and asked, "Did you poop in your underwear?"

He said, "Pooped in underwear. Pooped in underwear." Then he looked directly at me and said, "Ice cream is *bad*! Ice cream is *bad*!" Then he turned and walked away.

In that moment I realized my son talks exactly like Rain Man.

I also realized he must justify unpleasant situations in his mind. When he figures out he can't have something he wants, he will immediately turn that positive thing into something negative so it won't be as hard for him to deal with as it would be otherwise.

***

Journal Entry
March 2011
3 Years 7 Months Old

Like me and my siblings when we were young, Atticus has a habit of leaning backwards and trying to balance on two legs while sitting in the kitchen chair. No matter how many times I tell him to stop, I catch him in the act several times a day. Thankfully, he has a child-size kitchen table and chair he uses, so he is closer to the ground.

Today, I was checking my email at the kitchen counter when I heard an unusual thud. I turned around and saw Atticus lying belly-up like a turtle with the chair underneath his back. He appeared to be a little stunned as he lay motionless awaiting assistance.

I ran over to him and helped him up. I placed the chair under the table and asked, "How many times do I have to tell you to keep all four legs on the floor?"

He looked at me with a furrowed brow and said, "I only have two legs."

***

Journal Entry

October 2011

4 Years 2 Months Old

I go to our local recreation center to workout. The facility offers child-care services for children six and under. Atticus has been attending this playroom area for a couple of years, and the regular women who watch over him have grown to understand him and know what to expect from him.

Today, the regular workers were absent, and the playroom was being run by a woman who knew Atticus by name and face but never worked directly with him. I made sure Atticus knew her name, told him she would be taking care of him today, and left the room.

During my workout time, I walked toward a different area of the building and passed the employee at the vending machine. She smiled at me, and I asked, "How's he doing?"

She began by telling me how smart Atticus is and that she has never seen anything like him.

Then she told me that he "shocked" her when he wanted a new piece of paper to write on.

"How so?" I asked.

He told her, "I need a new one."

She told him he had plenty of room to keep writing.

He repeated, "I need a new one."

She told him again that he had room to write.

Then, instead of speaking, he wrote on the paper, "I NEED A NEW ONE," and showed her the paper.

At that point she got him a new sheet of paper, but it had "Staff Only" written on the front. Atticus told her, "No, that's for staff only."

She couldn't believe what was happening and was completely taken aback. She finally found him a blank sheet of paper to write on, and he was happy.

As she was telling me about their morning together, she seemed genuinely surprised, and completely amused, at the ability of this little boy.

***

Journal Entry

November 2011

4 Years 3 Months Old

Atticus and I recently read *If You Give a Mouse a Cookie*, and he loved the story. After reading the book, we discovered there are several more stories in the *If You Give…* series written by Laura Numeroff.

For the last two weeks, he repeatedly told me that he wants, *If You Give a Moose a Muffin, If You Give a Pig a Pancake,* and *If You Take a Mouse to the Movies*—in that order. I kept telling him that we will go to the library and see if they have those books. Today was the day and Atticus couldn't stop talking about our impending trip.

I believe in empowering children to speak up for themselves and ask for what they need. I was an extremely shy child, and interaction with anyone outside my immediate family was difficult for me. I often wonder how different my life would have been if I had been pushed to interact with others as a child. I don't want Atticus to suffer the same fate. At the same time, I'm also acutely aware of his social limitations being on the autism spectrum, so I am always trying to teach him how to communicate with others.

During the car ride to the library, I told him he would have to ask the librarian for the books. He responded, "I do not want to go to the library."

I told him that he would go, and he would ask.

I felt a little sad about his sudden reluctance to go to the library. I'm conscious of his inability to ask questions and communicate in that manner. I know how difficult speaking can be for him. I could sense his fear, but I was not going to let fear stop him. Something inside told me it was the right thing to do.

We continued our drive to the library.

Once we arrived inside the building, we made our way to the children's area. As we approached the information desk, he was holding my hand, and I was gently reminding him that everything would be all right, and all he had to do was ask them for the books.

When we reached our destination, there were three librarians at the desk—two were standing and one was sitting in a chair. I saw a sign on the desk and asked Atticus, "What does the sign say?"

Hello, My Name Is Awesome

He read the sign, "Ask here."

I whispered in his ear, "Ask for the books." Atticus just stood there looking at the librarian sitting in the chair.

After a moment of silence, one of the librarians asked, "Can we help you?"

He had no idea how to ask them for the books, so I had to help him.

I softly said into his ear, "Say 'Do you have…'"

Atticus repeated super loud, "DO YOU HAVE?"

Then I whispered, "Tell them the books you want."

Atticus continued, "*If You Give a Moose a Muffin, If You Give a Pig a Pancake, and If You Take a Mouse to the Movies.*"

I was so thankful and proud in that moment. I was holding back tears as I looked up at the three women behind the desk. All of them had a look on their faces like they had just witnessed the most precious moment in history. The two standing slowly backed away as they looked at him and smiled from ear to ear. The one sitting in the chair said, "That is the most adorable thing I have ever seen. If that isn't an advertisement for the public library nothing is. Let's go see what we can find!"

I think this was the sweetest moment I have witnessed with him to date. I'm so proud of him and extremely thankful for the progress he has made so far. I've watched God work miracles in this sweet boy's life.

***

Journal Entry
November 2011
4 Years 3 Months Old

Atticus began participating in his first year of AWANA in the Cubbies department at our church this past September. AWANA is a program that helps children learn about God and His son, Jesus Christ.

Children receive handbooks that contain Bible lessons, Scriptures that are to be memorized by the child, and tasks that need completed. There are twenty-six lessons called Bear Hugs in the Cubbies book. The child can complete one each week or work at a slower pace if necessary.

Atticus loves Cubbies! He spends quite a bit of time at home with his nose in the pages of his handbook. Each week he writes the Scripture he needs to memorize on his chalkboard and reads his lesson. He was blessed with an excellent memory, so memorization comes easily for him. I help him with the extra credit tasks and read the stories with him to help give him a better understanding of what he is reading.

He just completed Bear Hug 7 in his handbook.

Today, I gave him yogurt and fruit to eat for an afternoon snack. He ate all the fruit, but he wouldn't touch the yogurt. I told him that he would have to stay in his seat, at the table, until he ate his yogurt.

He sat at the table without eating for about fifteen minutes when he suddenly said, "I want Mommy to feed me."

I said, "No."

I told him that he would have to feed himself.

More time went by, and he told me a few more times that he wanted me to feed him. I was growing impatient, so I said, "You'll sit there all day if need be. You'll feed yourself."

He tried to get up several times, but I stopped him before his bum was a couple of inches off the seat. He eventually gave up and didn't try to stand anymore.

We continued to go back and forth.

"Eat, Atticus."

"I want Mommy to feed me."

"Eat, Atticus."

"I want Mommy to feed me."

On and on we went for fifty-two long, miserable minutes.

Then, from out of nowhere, Atticus said, "Children obey your parents in the Lord. That is Bear Hug 22."

His words captivated me. First, he had just finished Bear Hug 7. How could he have Bear Hug 22 memorized? Secondly, he demonstrated that he completely understood that he was being disobedient, and he connected the situation back to Scripture. Incredible!

I didn't know whether he was correct about the Bear Hug, but this is Atticus. The kid has amazed me with his memorization skills in the past, so I wasn't going to argue with him. Instead, I said, "You know what? I'm going to check the handbook, and if that's Bear Hug 22, I'll feed you."

I found the book, turned the pages to Bear Hug 22, and sure enough, he was absolutely correct. I sighed in disbelief. I couldn't believe he had memorized Scripture from a future lesson and connected it to our current circumstance.

When I told him he was correct, he sat at the table and smiled at me. I could tell he was pleased with himself.

I fed him. He ate the yogurt. We *finally* got on with our day.

***

Journal Entry
July 2012
4 Years 11 Months Old

Atticus is terrified of water. Showers are a nightmare in our home—complete with screaming, crying, and a lot of yelling. He doesn't like the feel of soap on his hands, and he doesn't like water to touch his face or ears. We have resorted to using a sun visor in the shower when washing his hair to try and keep water away from his eyes, nose, and mouth. I loathe washing his hair, and I grow impatient with him during the process.

He told me he wants to take swimming lessons this summer. I, of course, argued that he can't even get his hair washed without screaming from irrational fear, so how on earth is he going to swim? He insisted that he would do better in a pool. I finally relented and paid for five lessons.

The first day of lessons I talked with the instructor and let her know about his fear and that he was on the autism spectrum but high functioning. She was very warm and accepting.

As she led the group toward the pool, Atticus was very cautious about going in the water, hesitating and walking slowly. He was well behind his group as they made their way to their designated area in the pool.

When he finally caught up to them, I watched as all the other boys in his group submerged their entire body in the water. Meanwhile, Atticus stood waist-deep in the water and gently moved his hands from side-to-side. I watched as the other boys mimicked a swimming motion while lying on their bellies in the shallow end of the pool. Atticus just stood there looking terrified. To his credit, he didn't cry or scream.

I must be honest. I was frightened. As I watched him walking around inside the pool, I was scared to death that he would fall and go under. I had no idea if he would be able to hold his breath or not.

The first lesson ended without incident, and we all considered it a success because he was able to bend over and get his mouth close enough to the water to blow bubbles.

We came back the second day and it was more of the same. I could see his instructor trying to coax him into attempting certain things, but he wasn't having any of it.

After the lesson, the instructor came over to me and told me that Atticus really didn't want to do much today. She said she thought he was really cute though, and she tried to get him to try several new things, but he declined each one.

She provided several suggestions, but Atticus told her, "I do not like the water. I do not like to swim. I do not like to get my hair wet."

The instructor offered him one final option and said, "Let's go over to the blue slide."

Atticus said, "I do not like the blue slide."

Annoyed, she asked, "Atticus, what do you like?"

He stopped and thought about it for a second and then said, "I like myself."

***

Journal Entry
May 2013
5 Years 9 Months Old

Atticus has lost quite a few teeth lately. Tonight, he displayed an unusual interest in his missing teeth, and he told me that he is missing three now—one front tooth, one on the back-left side, and one on the back-right side. I told him that the adult teeth would come through when he is older.

His eyes widened at the thought, and he said, "Those ones, I think, they're stuck in my throat!"

***

Hello, My Name Is Awesome

Journal Entry

April 2014

6 Years 9 Months Old

There's been a huge swing in Atticus's behavior lately—and not for the better. There are times when my sweet boy turns into a little monster I don't recognize.

He has taken to arguing with me, questioning everything I ask him to do, and generally being defiant in ways I didn't know he was capable of. Still, I try to be thankful that he's asking questions—even in the midst of a barrage of obnoxious queries when I tell him to do something as simple as take his plate to the sink.

I've noticed this change developing gradually over this school year, and I tend to blame myself. My decision to send him to a school geared solely toward autistic children has exposed him to both mild and severe behavioral issues daily. Atticus has always been a child who picks up on certain behaviors of other children and mimics them.

In his second year of special-needs preschool, one of his classmates had a disability and made certain vocal noises throughout the day. Atticus picked up on the sound and would come home and make the humming, semi-grunting noise all the time—I mean constantly. When I asked him why he was making the sound, he told me they are, "Joe noises." No matter how often I told him to stop, he wouldn't.

I finally spoke to his teacher about this behavior, and she noticed him making the sounds at school as well. The teacher spoke to Atticus about it and explained that those sounds belong to Joe, not Atticus. I think it helped curb the behavior at school, but it didn't stop at home for over a year. To this day, if he hears the name Joe, he makes the noise.

So, understanding that Atticus mimics behaviors, and realizing that he witnesses unseemly conduct at school most days, I slowly realized that being with children who have behavioral problems for four days a week, six hours a day, might be affecting him.

Atticus didn't seem bothered by any of the drama the first part of the school year, but as the year is winding down, he's developed a sense that if he screams enough, or cries enough, or argues enough, he will get his way in all things. He is wrong.

I've lived with his irrational thought processes and meltdowns long enough to know that this recent behavior is different. This kid is smart, and I believe he's begun using the behavior he witnesses at school to get his way at home. I refuse to play that game. And that truth, I'm sure, is going to be the death of me.

Today was unfathomable. As I write this, I can't even begin to explain how the ordeal began, but I can say the resulting conflict was unlike anything the two of us have experienced thus far.

Atticus wouldn't stop arguing with me no matter what I said or did. Eventually, his constant arguing turned to moments of anger, then sadness, then back to arguing again. In his moments of sadness, I tried to calm him with hugs. That always works. It didn't work. I tried to sooth him with soft-spoken words. That usually works. It didn't work. His emotions and behavior intensified as the moments wore on.

I finally reached a point where I couldn't take the yelling, screaming, and crying any longer, so the punishments began and ended as follows: He's not allowed to play with the Kindle for seven days—didn't work. He isn't allowed to watch his favorite game show next week—didn't work. I gave him two swift, open-hand smacks on his rear-end. That got his attention, and he realized he needed to take me a little more seriously.

I told him to go to his bedroom where he could scream all he wants, but he wasn't to leave his room until he calmed down. He stomped up the stairs, screaming the entire way. I heard the bedroom door slam and muffled screams forced their way down the stairway to my aching ears. I fell back in my chair to surrender my mounting anger to the Lord.

Eventually, Atticus calmed down enough to come back downstairs. I brought him to me and hugged him. I tried to explain that he can't continue to talk back to me and be as defiant as he has been.

I asked him if he loved me.

He responded, "My voice box doesn't work."

I couldn't help but laugh. I turned my head away from him so he wouldn't see me grin. When I regained my composure, I told him, "I love you."

     Hello, My Name Is Awesome

He said, "I love you too."

After a few hugs and kisses, we were able to continue our day—even though it was a little more somber than before.

Later this evening, Atticus was upset again. He moaned about everything and seemed genuinely sad. Perhaps he wasn't completely recovered from all the ugliness earlier in the day.

I sat him on my lap and patted his back. He finally stopped crying and was calm enough to talk.

Trying to put a light-hearted spin on the moment, I asked, "What's the problem? Are you growing? Does your belly hurt? Is your brain okay? Do you need to see a psychiatrist?"

He said, "I'm growing too much, and I'm very young."

His words touched my heart.

Oh, sweet child, I pray I'll always remember you're young and the struggles you face as you grow, learn, and navigate your way through life. Please forgive my impatient nature and love me despite my many flaws.

***

Journal Entry
July 2014
6 Years 11 Months Old

How important is the library and reading to Atticus? So important that he thinks taking away that privilege is a punishment if you do something wrong.

We were traveling home from a day trip with a friend and her daughter, who is a few years older than Atticus. The daughter was mad at her mom over a food choice at a fast food restaurant we had just left, and she refused to answer her mother when spoken to.

After the mom's repeated attempts failed to get a response from her daughter, Atticus decided to intervene.

He kept telling the daughter to, "Answer your mother! Answer your mother! You need to answer your mother!"

Each time Atticus became more aggravated that she wouldn't respond. After several attempts, he finally bellowed, "When are you going to talk to your mom? Stop ignoring her, or she'll get angry and take your library card forever!!!!"

His words broke the silence, and everyone in the car chuckled.

***

Journal Entry
March 2015
7 Years 7 Months Old

I was preparing to brush Atticus's teeth tonight when something got in his eye. He jerked his head, rubbed his eye, and stomped his feet.

"Is something in your eye?" I asked.

He screamed, "AAAAAAAAAAAAAAAHHHHHHHHHHH-HHHHHH!!!! Maybe a giant piece of bark!! Or a fly got in my eye and died!!!!"

The pesky culprit was never discovered.

***

Journal Entry
December 2015
8 Years 4 Months Old

Atticus and I were browsing the office supply aisle at Walmart this evening. I had just found the bulletin board I wanted to buy when Atticus asked, "Mommy, is that a muzzle?"

My eyes followed the direction of his pointing finger where I discovered a two-year-old girl sitting in a cart. Smiling, I said, "No, that's a pacifier."

The child's mother burst out laughing and said, "It serves the same purpose! I can't wait to tell my mom about this."

***

Journal Entry
Dec 2017
10 years old

"I don't want to ruin the fun," he said. "But I have questions."

I picked Atticus up at school today. As we were walking to the car, he told me that a classmate said that Santa isn't real. I asked him what he

Hello, My Name Is Awesome

thought. He didn't answer. We continued to walk toward the car on this frigid, sunny day.

My mind drifted back to many of the fun, and often magical, Christmas memories we've shared together… That December when he wanted to visit as many Santa's as possible. We found St. Nick in some unsuspecting places. The year we met two Santa's at the exact same location at the exact same time – that was the year Atticus discovered that Santa has a lot of "helpers." The time Atticus insisted he had to dress as Rudolph to meet with Santa. And each year when my sweet child timidly approached the man in red and whispered his hopes and desires for Christmas morning.

It seems as though Atticus has always known that I'm the Easter bunny and the tooth fairy. I never hid it well. When asked, I answered, "Yes, I am." It didn't seem important to me to keep up the charade—but Christmas was different. Santa was different.

When he was younger, he asked about Santa, and my reply was, "The spirit of Santa is real and will live forever." He was happy with my answer and never asked again.

I suppose I enjoyed the wonder that sparkled in his eyes during the Christmas season, and I didn't want it to end. I savored the innocent belief of a child who trusted that a benevolent man magically delivered presents on the day we celebrate the greatest gift of all.

"I don't want to ruin the fun," he said. "But I have questions."

As we buckled our seat belts, I told him to ask his questions.

"Is Santa real?" He asked.

I didn't want to answer. I replied, as I did a few years earlier, "The spirit of Santa is real."

"But is Santa real?" He asked again.

"Are you sure you want me to answer?"

"Yes," he said.

I replied with the truth he was aching to hear, "I'm Santa."

His eyes wide with disbelief, and a forced smile on his face, he gently asked, "You're Santa? There isn't a Santa?"

"No."

"There isn't a Rudolph the Red Nosed Reindeer?"

"No."

"No Dasher, Dancer, Prancer, or Vixen?"

"No."

He continued to smile. "You go shopping by yourself and buy presents?"

"Yes."

After a few minutes, the thought that I was truly Santa began to sink in, and he realized that he had no hope of receiving the Xbox that he has longed for the last couple of years, or a six pack of Coca Cola which is his most recent desire. He hung his head in defeat. I couldn't help but chuckle.

I brought the conversation back to the spirit of Santa. I asked him what the spirit of Santa meant. He replied that it means "giving to others," which naturally led to a discussion about the child who was born to give His life for us all.

I was reminded that it doesn't matter if Atticus thinks Santa is real, or if he knows that the three presents under the tree each Christmas morning was paid for and wrapped by his mommy. He clearly understands the reason we celebrate this time of year. He knows the spirit of giving stems from the man who hung on a cross more than two thousand years ago—and that spirit is real and will live forever.

Chapter 9
All Things Presidential

My intent in writing this book is to inspire hope—not to be political. However, I can't write Atticus's story without including a few political anecdotes. Your own personal political leanings will determine whether you find them amusing.

Atticus was born into a home where politics was a popular topic of conversation. Both his father and I have specific political leanings, so we pay attention to the goings-on in Washington DC as well as the world around us. We do our best to be civic-minded citizens by staying informed of the current happenings in our government and to vote accordingly.

Atticus naturally took to our political musings and began attending events like his first political rally when he was one year old. He has attended several rallies since, and he loves to meet politicians and have his picture taken with them.

When Atticus was about eighteen months old, he discovered a presidential placemat that I had bought a few years prior to his birth. I'm not sure where he found the placemat as I had forgotten about it until his little feet walked it over to me one afternoon.

He handed the placemat to me and pointed to the first picture on the top left. I soon realized that he wanted me to tell him who the person was, so I told him it was George Washington. He was thrilled with this information. Smiling ear to ear and looking at me with eager blue eyes, he pointed to the second guy in line and anticipated my response. "John Adams," I said. Happiness beamed across his angelic face. Then he pointed to the third guy, and I informed him it was Thomas Jefferson. We continued this process until every single man on the placemat was named, concluding with George

W. Bush. Atticus was thrilled! He wanted to do it all again, so he pointed at Washington one more time.

It was in that moment he discovered one of his earliest obsessions—Presidents of the United States.

It soon became apparent how much Atticus loved this placemat filled with pictures of perfect strangers—and his obsessive and repetitive nature soon intruded on my time and energy. Every day he brought the placemat to me, pointed to each picture in the order they appeared, and I had to say each man's name aloud—multiple times. It only took me a couple of days to tire of this exercise, but he was just getting started.

A couple of weeks in, I remembered a deck of presidential picture cards I purchased a few years earlier from a child selling school fund-raising items door to door. I put the cards in my junk drawer and forgot about them. Out of sheer boredom, I decided to introduce the cards to Atticus instead of going over the placemat again.

The cards were a huge success. However, the cards didn't cause the demise of the placemat as I had hoped. They simply complimented the presidential process.

Our new routine included both items and went as follows: Atticus pointed to the presidents on the placemat, I said the name, he found the card that matched the name, and then lay the cards, in sequential order, on the floor around the placemat.

My mind went numb around the second time of doing this each day. I inevitably told him I was finished and got up and walked away. He signed "more" to let me know he wanted me to continue to play, but I told him to play with the cards by himself. He always carried on without me. I'm confident he was mentally saying the name of each president as he continued the process alone in silence.

By the time July rolled around, we were engaging in our presidential playtime a few times a week rather than a few times per day. On July 2nd, a month and a half before he was to turn two, he brought the placemat to me and pointed to George Washington. On that particular day, I didn't feel like performing the same old routine. Instead of speaking aloud the name "George Washington," I looked at Atticus and asked, "Where is Abraham

Hello, My Name Is Awesome

Lincoln?"

He tilted his head and looked at me. He was probably thinking, *That isn't how this game is played, Mommy!* Then, to my surprise, he looked at the placemat and pointed to Abraham Lincoln.

I wasn't sure how to react. Of course, I thought he was learning the names of each of the men in the pictures, although I wasn't certain since he couldn't speak to communicate any information, but I never considered he would be able to point to the picture of a name I gave him—out of successive order no less.

I said, "Good job!"

He smiled and waited for me to announce another name. I wondered if this was a fluke. I decided to test him. "Atticus, where is George Washington?"

He pointed to George Washington.

"Good job!"

He was enjoying every minute of our new game.

"Where is Ronald Reagan?"

He pointed to Ronald Reagan.

I called my mom to inform her of this new development. She said I needed to test him with more obscure presidents—as if that made a difference to an almost two year old. All presidents are obscure to two year olds! But in that moment, I wasn't thinking logically. I was thinking like my mom—*She's right, everyone knows those presidents.*

So we went the more obscure route.

"Where is Ulysses S. Grant?"

He pointed to Ulysses S. Grant.

"Where is William Howard Taft?"

He pointed to William Howard Taft.

"Where is Franklin Pierce?"

He pointed to Franklin Pierce.

No matter what name I said that day, or what order I called them in, he pointed to the correct president every single time. He had a blast with our newfound way of playing the president game.

****

Atticus also has a love of geography. Armed with this knowledge, my mom bought him a magnetic map of the United States for his second birthday. We put the map on the refrigerator.

A few weeks later, I was browsing a bookstore and found a book about presidents of the United States. The book included all presidents at the time of printing—George Washington through George W. Bush. It contained pictures, brief personal biographies, presidential accomplishments, wars, failures, electoral map information, and the printed inauguration speech of each president. I thought it would be a wonderful gift for Atticus when he was older, so I bought it.

When I arrived home, I decided to show Atticus the book, and he was ecstatic! He took the book out of my hands, put it on the floor, and browsed the pages. He refused to give it back. That book belonged to him now, and he was going to keep it.

On rare occasions we went through the same process with the book as we did with the cards and placemat—he pointed to the picture, and I said the name. At times he pointed to the statistical information provided in the book—the order of each presidency, hometowns, first ladies—and I read aloud what the text said.

He spent most of the time looking through the book on his own because I had long since grown tired of all things presidential. There were days he spent two or three hours alone, sitting on the floor, browsing the pages. I can only imagine what was going on inside his mind.

One evening, a couple of months after receiving the book, I came home from a long day of running errands. Atticus and his dad met me at the door. His dad was excited to show me something.

He led me to the kitchen and said, "Watch this."

Atticus and his dad walked over to the table where Tim randomly opened the presidential book. The book opened to Jimmy Carter. Tim asked Atticus, "What state is Jimmy Carter from?"

Atticus hurried over to the refrigerator, where his magnetic map of the United States lived, pulled Georgia off the map, and brought the state back

Hello, My Name Is Awesome

to his dad.

Tim stared at me in disbelief. I'm sure my expression mirrored his.

I asked Tim if he had been practicing that. He said, "No. It just happened."

He explained that they were looking through the book, and he asked Atticus what state one of the presidents was from, and Atticus walked over to the map and came back with the correct state. This was obviously Atticus's way of answering the question because he couldn't answer using words.

I called out a couple of names to see if Atticus knew the state. "George W. Bush."

Atticus went to the refrigerator and retrieved the Texas part of the map.

"Ronald Reagan."

Atticus returned with California.

"Abraham Lincoln."

Atticus came back with Illinois.

I decided to throw him a curveball, so I said, "Elvis Presley."

He returned with the Tennessee magnet. We're huge Elvis fans, so the kid knew Elvis was from Tennessee.

Suddenly, I realized my child not only knew all the presidents of the United States, but he also knew where every single state in the union was located on the map—and he was only two.

In December of that same year, Santa brought Atticus an interactive presidential learning toy for Christmas. Of course, it was his favorite gift that year. He spent Christmas day sitting at the kitchen table, laying his head on the interactive board, pushing the buttons, and listening to all the information the strange electronic voice had to relay.

The toy was portable, so he carried it around the house and pushed the buttons whenever he felt like hearing the information it provided. He always seemed to have that toy with him no matter where he went.

I fell in love with the toy because it freed me from my misery of sitting and repeating the names of presidents.

Now Atticus was all set with his presidential arsenal—a placemat, cards, book, and an interactive toy. My mother even bought him a talking

Ronald Reagan doll that played actual Reagan sound bites when you pushed a button. The boy loved all of it!

I decided early on to be a mother who follows her child's lead when it comes to his interests and hobbies. Atticus has always been a child with unusual interests for his age, and I felt as if I would be doing him a disservice if I tried to steer him in a different direction than he was naturally inclined to go—even if others thought it inappropriate. My standard was, "Is it illegal or immoral?" If the answer was no, then I couldn't see a reason not to support him in whatever area he took a fancy to.

Not everyone agreed with my parenting style. I remember working with his first speech pathologist early on. When her monthly visits to our home began, she made innocuous remarks regarding his presidential collection. I could tell right away that she was not amused with all the time Atticus spent "playing" with them.

As time went by, she became more blunt, saying such things as, "You are aware he doesn't know who the presidents are." And, "He should be learning this stuff in fifth grade, not when he's two."

I responded that he enjoys playing with them, and I see no reason not to let him have his fun.

She was trying to encourage me to force more age-appropriate items on him, but he never took much interest in age-appropriate things, and I certainly wasn't going to deprive my child of something that brought him such joy. I began hiding his book and interactive toy when it was time for her to visit, so we could avoid the topic all together. An added bonus was that it helped him focus more on his session with her.

***

I look back on those days with both fond and not so fond memories. As I sit here writing his story, I'm convinced I was his voice in those days.

Atticus had zero ability to speak the simplest of words, much less the names of presidents, but he desperately wanted to hear the names. That's why he constantly appealed to me for help with the vocalization. He obviously knew the name that went with every single picture, and he didn't need any help understanding, but what he did need was to hear the names spoken

     Hello, My Name Is Awesome

aloud. That was something he was incapable of doing, and he knew Mommy was there to help.

Having been blessed or cursed—depending on your view—with a mother who both loves and hates politics, and who tries to explain political situations to an extremely young child when asked, I don't think it's any surprise that Atticus's thoughts can promote political discussion from time to time.

And considering his fondness for the presidents themselves, it leaves little room to wonder why their names are always on his mind.

***

Journal Entry
January 2012
4 Years 5 Months Old

While Atticus was eating breakfast this morning, he was studying a map of the White House. He began flapping his hands with excitement and said, "I want to go into the White House when I'm older."

Before I could respond, he looked at me and said, "Maybe when I'm president."

***

Journal Entry
August 2012
5 Years Old

Atticus began a new year of preschool this week. This evening I asked him who his new friends are, and he replied, "I saw Grant today. Not President Grant because he is in heaven."

***

Journal Entry
November 2013
6 Years 3 Months Old

Atticus and I were watching Jeopardy this evening. My television viewing time is usually interrupted every couple of minutes because I have to continually tell him to get out from in front of the TV. He has a lot of energy, so it's the rare occasion when he will watch television without constantly moving around the room, plus he gets excited seeing the number and letter graphics that come with viewing the game show.

When the final Jeopardy question was asked, I heard Atticus say, "Millard Fillmore."

I didn't pay it any mind until Alex Trebek revealed the correct question was indeed, "Who is Millard Fillmore?"

I was stunned. I asked Atticus how on earth he knew the answer was Millard Fillmore. His only response was, "I don't know."

I can only surmise that he had just read that fact in his presidential book that he took off the shelf a few days earlier and began perusing again during breakfast each morning.

Oh, the final Jeopardy answer? "The second man to become president who was never elected to the job, he twice ran for the position unsuccessfully."

***

Journal Entry
January 2014
6 Years 5 Months Old

While riding in the car today, Atticus asked, "Who will be the forty-fifth President?"

I've been so disillusioned with our government the last few years that this was a topic I didn't want to discuss, so I responded, "I don't want to talk about it."

Atticus then declared, "I want to be president some day! I'm going to be president from 2081 to 2097. I'm going to die in office."

I didn't have the heart to explain he could only serve eight years.

***

Journal Entry
February 2014
6 Years 6 Months Old

As I was driving Atticus to school this morning, he tried to coax me into an argument regarding political parties, but I refused to take the bait.

This evening, he decided to revisit the conversation.

"I'm going to be a Democrat when I grow up," he said.

I told him he's too young to understand what Democrat and Republican means. He doesn't understand the price of freedom and the values this country was founded on. I explained to him that when he is older, I have plenty of books about liberty, the founding fathers, and the United States Constitution, and after he reads them, he can make his decision on what political party he wants to align himself with.

I completed my scant lecture by rhetorically asking, "Are you going to be a patriot and uphold the Constitution, or are you going to be an enemy of the Constitution?"

Atticus answered, "Enemy."

I was taken aback. Without thought, I replied, "Then you will no longer be my son."

Without missing a beat, Atticus looked at me, shrugged his shoulders, and said, "Anyway, you'll be dead when I'm president."

***

Journal Entry
March 2014
6 Years 7 Months Old

I'm often amused by the random thoughts Atticus will verbalize. Like other children, you never know what is going to come out of his mouth, but his thoughts seem to be on a different level than most. I regularly find myself asking the question, "Do other kids think like this?" Obviously, his brain processes thoughts, ideas, and interests differently than most children, so I'm guessing the answer is no.

This morning, while I was preparing breakfast, all was quiet until Atticus blurted out, "Tim, who is considered my dad, was two years old when JFK was assassinated on the streets of Dallas Texas."

I looked up from the food I was preparing, completely thrown off by the words I just heard and the manner in which he spoke them. I instantly grabbed pen and paper to record his thought.

I was struck with the information he had just put forth, and somewhat astonished that a six-year-old would be sitting at the kitchen table, waiting for his breakfast, processing information such as the year his father was born, the location and year of a president's assassination, and calculating how old his dad was at the time of the assassination.

Once again, I found myself asking the question, "Do other kids think like this?"

***

Journal Entry
March 2014
6 Years 7 Months Old

We were riding in the car this morning when Atticus said, "When people die, I will get a rocket ship and take them to heaven. If people have something wrong with them, I will take them to heaven and see what Jesus can do."

I asked, "You're going to see what Jesus can do for them?"

"Yes, if something is wrong. Maybe if they have a stroke like Franklin D. Roosevelt or something."

***

Journal Entry
May 2014
6 Years 9 Months Old

Another random thought from Atticus: "When I get to heaven, I'll get to see lots of presidents. Even the one who died of pneumonia, William Henry Harrison."

***

Journal Entry
June 2014
6 Years 10 Months Old

A casual thought from Atticus while he was looking at a fifty-dollar bill: "Hi, Grant! If you were alive today, which you are not because you lived in the 1870s, I would be rooting for you!"

***

Journal Entry
August 2014
A Few Days Shy of 7 Years Old

On the way home from school today, Atticus declared, "I don't want to go to school anymore."

He's only four days into the new school year, so I asked, "Already? Why?"

"It's boring," he said. "I want to be homeschooled and travel the world! I wish I lived at Monticello!"

Monticello is the home of Thomas Jefferson. Atticus was born with a traveling bone and will travel anywhere at the drop of a hat, but presidential homes are of great interest to him. He may not ever be able to live at Monticello, but I hope someday to take him to visit the historical site.

Unfortunately for him, I don't have the ability, or financial means, to homeschool him and travel the world.

***

Journal Entry
March 2015
7 Years 7 Months Old

While sitting at the table eating dinner with my sweet, beautiful Atticus this evening, he broke the silence and stated matter-of-factly, "When you had me, you were as fat as William Howard Taft."

Pause.

Where did that come from? I didn't ask, but I'm thinking if this kid has a prayer of getting a girl when he's older, he best start working on his communication skills with the opposite sex.

For the record, I wasn't that fat.

***

Journal Entry
April 2015
7 Years 8 Months Old

Atticus and I love to travel and visit presidential homes. So far, we've visited the homes of William Howard Taft, Warren Harding, and Benjamin Harrison. Our hope is to visit all existing presidential homes within the continental United States. This endeavor will take quite a few years, but we are excited and hopeful at the prospect.

Atticus can be engaging at times and most adults seem to be drawn to his personality. It doesn't hurt that he comes armed with facts that most children his age don't know, and he isn't afraid to talk and lead conversations. Most tour guides we have encountered take to him easily and seem to enjoy the time they spend with him.

Today we travelled to the home of Rutherford B. Hayes in Fremont, Ohio. Upon entry to the home, the tour guide greeted me and Atticus and another family of four.

While the tour guide was introducing himself, Atticus raised his hand to speak. Sometimes it can be difficult for Atticus to restrain himself from talking, but he's working hard to learn how to control his impulse to speak when he's in a public setting such as this.

After the tour guide completed his introduction, he pointed to Atticus and gave him permission to talk.

Atticus said, "This is Rutherford B. Hayes's house. He was born in Delaware, Ohio ... This is the first time I've been to a president's home since I went to Benjamin Harrison's house in Indianapolis, Indiana. Mom and I are going to visit every president's house except one—Barack Obama's."

Atticus paused to take a breath. All the adults in the room were smiling and looked at me without saying a word. They quickly turned their attention back to Atticus, and the tour guide asked him why we wouldn't be visiting Barack Obama's house.

Atticus explained, "Because he lived in Hawaii, and he spent his boyhood on another continent in Kenya!"

Laughter ensued as they all found Atticus's knowledge and delivery to be amusing. I'm confident everyone present was glad to be there that day.

Hello, My Name Is Awesome

Chapter 10
Math Whiz

Between the ages of one and two, I realized that I wasn't dealing with a typical toddler. Little by little Atticus's personality, interests, and knowledge revealed themselves, and they often amazed me.

My experience with children was limited at the time, but I was pretty sure he was different than most kids. My mother's wonderment to each new Atticus story I shared confirmed my suspicions. After all, she raised three children, so she should know.

His love for the alphabet, books, and magazines was apparent early on. I'm absolutely convinced that he recognized words when he was as young as seventeen months old—possibly younger.

His fascination with the alphabet was obvious to anyone who spent time with him. We had a magnetic alphabet set on a whiteboard that he spent an enormous amount of time looking at each day. He always made sure we spent a little time together reviewing each letter. Our routine resembled our presidential playtime in a lot of ways; the only difference was the subject matter.

Atticus also taught me that certain letters can be different letters if turned upside down or on their side. For example, the letter "N" is a "Z" if turned on its side. The letter "d" is a "p" if turned upside down. The letter "u" is an "n" turned upside down.

I never examined the alphabet in that manner, so I was dazzled when he brought those letters to me and had me say the name of the letter aloud while he held it in its natural position. Then he turned the letter to make a new one and waited for me to say the new name. When I realized what he was doing, he squealed with joy. He fascinated me.

Because he enjoyed the ABCs so much, I bought him a pack of alphabet flash cards. Each card had the upper-and-lower-case letter along with a picture and a word that began with that letter. Atticus loved those cards! He made me say each letter and word aloud to him at least once a day for weeks. When I was feeling charitable, I would review the set twice. He spent a generous amount of time playing alone with the cards, which allowed me time to catch up on housework.

Atticus was entranced with the alphabet, and he often attempted to create the sound each letter made, but he was never able to produce the correct sound. For example, his "c" sound would be a cough. Yes, a literal cough. Every time he saw the letter "c" he coughed. His "b" sound was "day." His "h" sound was "huh huh." Other than trying to articulate the sound each letter makes and trying to imitate sounds such as sirens or animal noises—which he didn't imitate correctly either—he never attempted to communicate using words or any type of vocalization.

I distinctly remember going through our home and cleaning one afternoon. Atticus was sixteen months old and sitting in his highchair near the kitchen table. I passed him every time I had trash to put in the garbage can.

I eventually passed him with a couple of health and fitness magazines in my hand. They were a few months old, so I decided I no longer wanted them. As soon as I put them in the trash can, Atticus screamed and didn't stop. I had no idea what happened as he was enjoying himself and seemed content up to that point.

I ran over to him, asking, "What's wrong? What's wrong?" The more I asked, the louder he screamed. It didn't take long before the tears began to flow. Then I noticed his right hand was reaching in the direction of the trash can.

He couldn't speak, so he didn't answer my question verbally, but he kept reaching toward the trash can while crying. *He can't be upset because I threw away some magazines.*

Nevertheless, I listened to my gut. I walked over to the trash can, opened the lid, pulled out the magazines, and then held them up. "Do you want these?" I asked.

The sight of the months-old publications soothed him. His deafening cries turned to slightly audible breathes as he recovered from his emotional torment—but he kept reaching.

I walked back to his chair and handed the magazines to him. He smiled, took the magazines from me, put them on the highchair tray, and contently browsed the pages.

This was one of the weirdest moments I witnessed in those early days. He was less than two years old and having a meltdown over a magazine. I wasn't surprised though. As I watched him happily examine each page, I knew it was part of who he is. I wasn't in denial.

We woke up one morning, and I didn't want to be bothered with the alphabet again. It takes a lot of patience to do the same boring routine every single day, and I needed a break.

It sounds strange, but I got to the point where my brain felt detached when I had to repeat letters and presidential names. My mind wasn't connected to my body any longer—just floating around somewhere in space—completely disconnected from my reality. I found myself stretching out on the floor, staring at the ceiling, and wishing I never had to see another letter or president as long as I live. So, occasionally, I tried to think of something to shake-up our routine.

On this particular day, I decided to introduce Atticus to the number magnets that came with the alphabet set. For some reason I stored them away instead of giving them to him.

I thought I was going to teach him numbers that morning. I was wrong. Instead of learning numbers, Atticus showed me that he already knew them.

How do I know? I know because I poured the bag full of numbers onto the kitchen floor and asked Atticus, "Can you bring me the number one?"

He brought me the number one. Then I asked him for the number two. He brought me the number two. This continued until he brought me all the numbers—zero through nine.

I have no idea where he learned the name of each number. I never intentionally sat down with him to teach him prior to that day. He didn't find the numbers and bring them to me like he did the letter magnets or the presidential placemat. No, in this case I presented the numbers to him, and he already had a working knowledge of them. I'm still not sure how or where he learned them—perhaps a book we read?

His love of numbers was strong and became more apparent as he aged and was able to communicate verbally. To me it appeared that his penchant for numbers was inherent—a God given ability that came naturally to him. This has been one of the most astounding things to witness as he continues to grow. He simply amazes me at times.

When he was four years old, I passed his bedroom door and heard him lying on his bed counting. I decided to stop and listen. He was counting by ones, and I wanted to see how high he could go. I patiently listened outside his door while he continued to count all the way to five hundred without missing a number.

I was impressed. I soon discovered he was able to count by increments of twos, fives, tens, and twenties as well.

When he was five years old, he woke up one morning, and while lying in bed, he began counting by fives. I already knew he could count by the aforementioned increments, so I decided to see how far he could go. I asked him to count by thirties. He counted by thirties. I asked him if he could count by forties. He counted by forties. Then fifties. Then sixties. He was amazing me once again.

That evening, I shared my new discovery with his dad. I asked Atticus to count incrementally again. His dad, of course, was blown away, and we were laughing about how ridiculous it all seemed.

After Atticus finished counting by sixties, I said, "He can probably count by seventies, but we didn't try that."

Atticus promptly responded, "One forty, two ten, two eighty."

I happened to catch this moment on video, and shared it with his preschool teacher, Mrs. Downing, who enjoyed hearing about our discoveries.

As of this writing, Atticus works twice a week with an enrichment teacher at the Christian school he attends. She has confirmed his mathematical abilities and said that he has an "incredible number sense…strong computation skills…" and has demonstrated "…interest in mathematical reasoning…"

Atticus does, however, experience difficulty with certain aspects of math. His enrichment teacher relayed, "He has such an incredible number sense that he has not learned the strategies others need to do what he does so easily…he needs those [strategies] to move ahead into more difficult topics. He is also not very flexible in his thinking, wanting to use the algorithm he knows rather than looking for other connections or strategies. However, to his credit, he will listen when I try to point out a new strategy and because he is so good at remembering things, I feel confident that he will pick up these new ideas. Observing his sensitive nature, I think it is difficult for him to take a challenge and try something new when he thinks he might fail. We are working on understanding that learning comes from failures."

Once again God has been faithful where this child is concerned. He continues to place people in our lives who have the patience and ability to not only see Atticus's potential, but also are willing to go that extra mile to help him meet and exceed any and all possibilities he may possess inside him.

***

Journal Entry
October 2012
5 Years 2 Months Old

While preparing lunch this afternoon, Atticus exclaimed, "I want one trillion dollars!"

I told him I would like one trillion dollars as well.

He explained that he wants one trillion dollars so he can travel to Italy.

I said, "It doesn't cost one trillion dollars to go to Italy. It would only cost around ten thousand dollars."

Without missing a beat, Atticus questioned, "One hundred one hundred dollars?"

I stopped to think about what he was asking. *One hundred one hundred dollars?*

I grabbed a calculator to make sure. Yes, sure enough, 100 x $100 = $10,000.

***

Journal Entry
October 2012

5 Years 2 Months Old

While out in public places, Atticus will start conversations with adults because he is naturally friendly and inquisitive about subjects that interests him. After talking with Atticus for a couple of minutes, the adult will ultimately look at the parent Atticus is with and remark how smart he is.

When Atticus's dad is with him, he springs into action and asks Atticus questions such as, "What is the capital of Illinois? What is the capital of Florida? Who was the sixth President of the United States?" He's a proud father who likes to show off his kid's knowledge to anyone who will take the time to watch and listen.

I witnessed this firsthand recently, and I had to stop his dad from asking Atticus questions so the polite woman, who was stuck listening, could go about her business. I can only imagine how long it goes on when I'm not around.

This evening, Atticus and his dad went to a store that sells backyard sheds. Atticus began conversing with the store's owner. Eventually, their chat led to a game of *Name that State Capital* and *Name that President*.

As the owner continued to question Atticus, she grew more and more impressed with his knowledge. She was so surprised that he answered all her questions correctly that she decided to reward him.

She told him that she had a prize for him and handed him three one-dollar bills, to which Atticus replied, "I like pennies."

***

Journal Entry
December 2012
5 Years 4 Months Old

It's Christmas time! We were travelling down the road today when the song *A Wonderful Christmas Time* came on the radio.

Atticus asked, "Who is that?"

I answered, "Paul McCartney."

Atticus said, "He's one fourth of the Beatles."

What? Now you're doing fractions? You're only in preschool!

***

 Hello, My Name Is Awesome

Journal Entry
December 2012
5 Years 4 Months Old

While riding in the car, Atticus observed, "My birthday eve is August 22nd. I wasn't around on my birthday eve in 2007."

You're a brilliant young boy, my child.

****

Journal Entry
February 2013
5 Years 6 Months Old

From out of the blue, Atticus informed me, "One quarter of a minute is fifteen seconds."

Yes, he's doing fractions.

****

Journal Entry
March 2013
5 Years 7 Months Old

While eating breakfast this morning, Atticus announced, "In eleven and three-quarter hours, I get the computer."

I looked at the clock, and it read 8:15 a.m. He gets the computer each evening at 8:00 p.m.

****

Journal Entry
September 2013
6 Years 1 Month Old

I don't have the ability to explain Atticus's connection with complete strangers. It's something you have to witness to fully understand. No matter where we go, he always seems to make an impact on someone.

After church this afternoon, he and I went to an Italian restaurant for lunch. The server, Shawn, immediately took a liking to Atticus. So much so, that she decided to sit down at our table to have a conversation with him.

Atticus's first question to her was, "How old are you?"

She told him she was born February 22, 1978.

She began to talk about something else when Atticus interrupted her and excitedly said, "You are 35 years old!"

Shawn looked at him, shocked, and said, "Yes, I am!"

Then Atticus asked, "How old is your mom?"

Shawn told him, "My mom was born on my birthday, February 22, 1956. She's 22 years older than me…"

Atticus interrupted and exclaimed, "Your mom is 57 years old!"

Shawn was laughing at this point, and with wide eyes exclaimed, "Yes, she is!"

Atticus asked, "How old is your grandma?"

Shawn explained that her grandma died a few years ago but told Atticus that she was born January 29, 1929. She told him that since he was able to figure out how old she and her mom are, now he can figure out how old her grandma would be if she was still living.

Shawn then tried to talk to me about Atticus, when he interrupted again and said, "Oh, excuse me! Your grandma would be 84 years old!"

At that point, Shawn the server was so overwhelmed with Atticus's abilities that she laughed and said, "You're ridiculous! I have to leave this table!"

Atticus mentally calculated each answer within a few seconds of receiving the information.

Before we left, Shawn made Atticus promise to come back again and make sure he gets her for a server.

***

Journal Entry

September 2013

6 Years 1 Month Old

Atticus has been asking people their age for some time now. I've tried to correct this curious behavior on several occasions, but I've been unsuccessful so far. It doesn't help that most everyone will say, "Oh, that's okay," and then tell him their age as I'm trying to correct him. So he continues to

     Hello, My Name Is Awesome

ask everyone.

Today, we went to the Olive Garden for lunch. Atticus and our female server were engaging in conversation when he asked her, "How old are you?"

The server didn't answer immediately, giving Atticus enough time to say, "You gotta be 45 or more."

I buried my face in my hands. I was embarrassed as I looked up and saw the horror on the server's face.

Looking down at the ground, she quietly said, "I'm 45. How did you know that?"

I apologized to the server and told Atticus again that he shouldn't ask people their age. She assured me that it was all right, but I could tell as soon as he asked the question that she didn't want to reveal her age, and she certainly wasn't pleased with his guesswork.

***

Journal Entry
April 2014
6 Years 8 Months Old

While shopping at Giant Eagle, Atticus and I had to use the restroom. I allowed him to go first and then had him stand outside my stall, with feet in front of the stall door, while I used it.

As I was going about my business, I heard him say, "Are you 82 years old?"

I hung my head and felt helpless.

Then I heard an older woman's voice sound surprised and impressed. "I'm 86 years old!" she happily answered. "How did you get so smart?"

I tried to put myself back together as quickly as possible because I didn't know where this conversation was going to lead. As she was doting over him and asking his age, I stepped out of the stall.

She smiled at me and asked, "Are you his mom?"

I answered in the affirmative.

She couldn't get over the fact that a six-year-old little boy guessed her approximate age. Then she asked me how he got so smart.

She turned her attention back to Atticus, and they talked for a while.

He asked her about her grandchildren, and great-grandchildren, and he wanted to know how old she was when they were born. She told him she couldn't remember how old she was, but she does have twins of her own that were born when she was 18 and the twins are now 68.

Atticus replied, "Wow! They are old!"

She laughed and patted his head. Then she smiled at me and said, "He is wonderful!"

That's my Atticus, spreading joy wherever he goes—even in public restrooms.

***

Journal Entry
May 2014
6 Years 9 Months Old

Atticus said, "Every 365 24 hours makes one year."

I can't argue with that.

***

Journal Entry
June 2015
7 Years 10 Months Old

Atticus has been eagerly anticipating a trip to King's Island this summer. Today, he and I traveled to the credit union to purchase tickets.

When we approached the counter, I asked the teller how much the tickets cost. She informed me that they were $40.50 each. She then told me there were other options that included all you can drink beverages. She left the counter to find the promotional pricing.

When the teller walked away, Atticus said, "We need $243.00."

I didn't know what he was talking about, so I asked, "Why do we need $243.00?"

He crinkled his nose and squinted his eyes as he looked at me. Annoyed, he said, "To go to Kings Island!"

I asked him how he knew that, and he told me the tickets are $40.50 and we have six people going.

Hello, My Name Is Awesome

"How did you just do that in your head so quickly?" I asked.

He replied, "I don't know."

***

Journal Entry

June 2015

7 Years 10 Months Old

Atticus likes to come into my room to sleep in the middle of the night. I always make sure he falls asleep in his own bed, but he inevitably winds up with me before the night is through.

He didn't start making his way to my room until he was four years old. He used to come in every night, around 1:00 or 2:00 a.m., and greet me with a hardy, "Hello!" His greeting always made me happy. Oh, how I miss those days.

Now, at seven years old, he no longer announces his entrance, but he still makes his way in just about every single night. I don't mind. I adore him, and I know I will miss it when he is older and no longer wants to be with his mommy.

We've been able to sleep in the last couple of weeks since school paused for the summer. This morning it was super early, and he woke me up by stirring around in bed. I prayed he wouldn't wake up as I wanted to go back to sleep.

He continued to stir. I continued to pretend to sleep.

A few moments of silence passed when he suddenly said, "Guess what?"

"What?" I murmured.

"There is 1,440 minutes in one day."

I didn't respond immediately because my brain was half asleep, and I was trying to figure out how he knew that—and why he was talking about it this early in the morning.

Then he said, "I just did that in my head."

"What? How?"

I was awake now. I grabbed the pen and paper on my nightstand and quickly did the multiplication to check his numbers. He was correct. When am I going to learn to accept he is right without doing the math myself?

Chapter 11
Jesus Made the Dirt

In the early summer of 2010, I heard a calling. I was bothered night and day. "Get your child in church." I kept feeling an internal nudge. Sometimes it felt like an elbow to the gut. The words continued to ring in my ear: "Get your child in church."

While saved since I was twenty-two years old, it had been years since I attended a church service. Through the years, I had grown weary of the feel-good gospel message heard in many churches, and I had a multitude of personal conflicts that discouraged my soul.

Still, the call didn't cease, "Get your child in church."

Since Atticus was three months old, I had been enduring a marriage that existed in the legal and financial realms only, so I was suffering from a lack of companionship and no one to share my desires and hopes for the future. On top of that, my shy and introverted nature, which has plagued me my entire life, continued to assault my confidence and independence. But despite my loneliness, lack of confidence, and shy nature, in July 2010 I decided to gather all my courage, map out places of worship in my area, and begin church shopping—alone.

The plan was to attend several churches, within ten to fifteen miles of my home, to figure out where each church stood biblically. I had to determine which church I could trust with my child's soul. I planned to visit each place once, then I would narrow down the list to the ones that looked promising after the initial visit. Once the final list was complete, I would attend the surviving churches several times before making my final decision.

The second church on my list seemed too good to be true on my first visit, so I decided to pop in the following Sunday instead of attending a new location.

The second visit was much like the first. I couldn't believe that I was actually sitting in the pews of a church where the pastor not only spoke the gospel truth of salvation, but also spoke of sin, repentance, and a new life in Christ.

There were altar calls after each Sunday morning sermon—for both the saved and unsaved. The pastor was unafraid to step on toes. I found that refreshing and far removed from the feel good "God is love" sermons I heard in so many other churches throughout the years. This was a church that dealt with the hard topics that most churches shy away from these days, and the leadership seemed to understand, saved or not, we are all imperfect humans.

After three months of attending this church, listening to their biblical teachings, and witnessing their behavior in an activity outside the church walls, I decided this was the church I would allow Atticus to attend. Even though I didn't know it at the time, this decision was also critical on my path to reconnecting with God and ultimately reviving my desire to have an intimate and loving relationship with my heavenly Father.

In October 2010, Atticus began attending children's church every Sunday morning, while I attended the adult service in the sanctuary. Atticus was just beginning to use a handful of words in a way that you could understand him, but he still struggled with language. Because of this, I was uncomfortable leaving him alone in a strange environment, but I'm glad I put my fears aside and listened to the calling that I now know was from God.

One of the Sunday school teachers kept telling me that she would love to have Atticus attend her Sunday school class for three year olds. The class preceded children's church, so Atticus and I eventually began attending both the 10:00 a.m. Sunday school hour and the 11:00 a.m. church service.

I stand in awe as I look back and see how God surrounded Atticus with gentle, kind, and nurturing women who loved and encouraged him in those early years. They not only loved him, but they recognized his strengths, value, and potential. They never tried to marginalize him or minimize his participation in the process, and I will forever be grateful to those Sunday morning servants.

Atticus took well to his new church routine. When he first began attending, he didn't have an official diagnosis of autism, so I didn't discuss autism with people inside the church caring for him. I just continued to parent him the way I had always done. I let the workers know he had trouble communicating, but I asked them to always include him in everything the rest of the class was doing.

Easter Sunday arrived a couple of months into our new routine. Since I was new to the church, I had no idea changes were going to take place that day in the children's department.

Our church's primary department is in the basement of the building. The area is divided into two main sections—one side for three to five year olds and the other side for six to eight year olds. Atticus was three and a half at the time.

When we arrived Easter morning, the department looked different. The area where Atticus normally attended Sunday School was closed off. I found out that all the children were going to stay in the six- to eight-year-old section that morning.

There were several people who volunteered to work that Sunday. Some of them were familiar to Atticus while others were not. I didn't think anything of it, so I kissed Atticus and told him I would see him after church. I had just turned my back on him and took a few steps out of the door when I heard him scream. I immediately identified a meltdown taking place.

He was loud, and when I walked back into the room, I saw him standing, red in the face, sobbing uncontrollably. No one knew what to do, and no one had any idea why it was happening.

I rushed over to him and asked him what was wrong. He sobbed, "Go to that room!!!!"

He pointed at the doors and repeated, "Go to that room!!!!"

I realized that he needed to be in the room he typically goes in for Sunday school. When he arrived that morning, he was expecting his normal routine, and he wasn't prepared for a change.

I told one of the workers that Atticus is used to being in the other room when he arrives on Sunday mornings, and the sudden change in his routine was upsetting him. She sent one of the teenage volunteers, who Atticus was familiar with, to his normal room with him until his teacher arrived.

I waited with him to make sure he was all right.

Upon entering the familiar area, Atticus calmed down, and the volunteer handed him a piece of paper and a pen so he could write. The process of writing and drawing maps soothes Atticus, and he frequently engaged in this activity during down-time at church when he was younger. I was able to leave without further problems.

Since that episode, I've been proactive in dealing with changes in his routine at church—and anywhere else.

Once a year, as the children age, they are transitioned to a new Sunday school class with a different teacher. I always make sure Atticus is aware of the change ahead of time. I remind him several times in the weeks leading up to the big day. If there is a change in location, we will talk about it beforehand. If a class needs to be interrupted for choir practice, we will talk about it beforehand.

I've learned that constant communication is the key. We haven't had any other issues with change in the church setting since I instituted this rule.

***

When Atticus was four and five years old, he participated in a church program for two years and loved it. When he entered kindergarten, he was slated to advance to the next level in the program, which meant he would leave the comfort and care of familiar people and head into unfamiliar territory with a new director.

I was fine with the prospect of it all. I simply prepared Atticus ahead of time that he would transfer to a new location, with a new director, when the program resumed in the fall.

It didn't go as smoothly as I had hoped.

As September approached, the new program season was on the horizon, and with it came the urging: "Volunteer to help." I ignored the call, but much like the whispers of "Get your child in church," the calling wouldn't halt, and I began hearing alarm bells of: "VOLUNTEER TO HELP!!"

A week before the program was to begin, I approached the sign-up table, registered Atticus, then reluctantly told the woman behind the table that I'd like to volunteer. In the nicest voice I could muster, I informed her that I don't really like working with children, but I'd be more than happy to help with the administrative duties if possible. I felt it best to be truthful. She said that would be fine, and they would find a place for me.

On the first night of the program, I was shown what my responsibilities would be, and then I watched as Atticus's new director met with the children and then began separating them by room color. Each room had a leader assigned to supervise and help the children with their weekly assignment. Atticus was sent to the purple room.

It was during this process that I began to realize why the incessant urging to volunteer wouldn't stop. I stood stunned as I watched Atticus be separated from the so-called typical children and isolated to the purple room that gradually filled full of children with obvious, and not so obvious, developmental issues. One by one they were relegated to the purple room. I couldn't believe what I was witnessing.

Atticus was six years old, and up to that point, no one had ever tried to marginalize him in such a manner. No one had ever tried to marginalize him period.

Atticus participated in gymnastics, tennis, swim lessons, and Safety Town classes with typically developing children without issue. We attended several theatrical plays, political rallies, and parades together. On day trips and vacations we visited museums, historic homes, and took train rides. Even his special-needs preschool was loaded with "typical" peers; otherwise, I wouldn't have allowed him to participate in that program for three years.

My logic was simple. The more I exposed him to ordinary life events, surrounded him with typical children, and allowed him to experience unfamiliar situations, the more elevated his thinking and ability to adjust to his environment would become.

I never once had a teacher, coach, or leader tell me I should think about placing him in a classroom for slow learners or the developmentally challenged. My experience was quite the opposite. Teachers, coaches, therapists, and church volunteers always provided unprompted feedback with glowing reports of what a pleasure Atticus was to have around and how kind, sweet, and smart he is.

As I stood in the church basement that evening, and continued to

 Hello, My Name Is Awesome

watch the separation of the perceived weak versus the perceived strong, I truly couldn't believe what I was seeing. My heart ached.

I decided not to say anything that evening. I've learned it's not always best to react immediately to emotional circumstances. Instead, I did the job I came to do, but I was simmering inside. I wanted to take some time to calm down and rationally think through the situation.

I spent the following week seeking composure and praying for clarity. And while I was yet undecided on how to best handle the situation, it became clear in week two why God placed me in this program—to make sure Atticus was treated with equal respect and dignity.

We arrived early Wednesday evening for week two. Atticus signed in then took a seat on the floor with all the other children. I was helping another volunteer with check-in as the children talked to each other while waiting for game time to begin at 7:00 p.m. There wasn't time for games in week one, so this was the first game night of the year.

Right before the fun was to begin, I saw Atticus, and all the children from the purple group, lined up and taken out of the game area by their room leader. I asked the volunteer sitting next to me if she knew where the worker was taking the kids. She informed me they were being taken downstairs to their room. I asked her why they weren't participating in game time with the other children, and she made mention of a decision by the director not to have them participate. This was the first I had heard about that decision.

My head felt like it was going to explode! First, Atticus was sent to the "special" room, and now he wasn't allowed to participate in game time. Was this really happening?

I found it hard to concentrate that evening. I was determined to speak with the director before I left that night. Unfortunately, time went by quickly, and it was so busy that I didn't get a chance to pull the director aside to talk. However, his wife was helping that evening, and I was able to pull her aside and talk to her. I told her, as nicely as possible, that I wasn't happy with Atticus being excluded from game time, or that he was relegated to the room with the "special" kids. Her response was, "Well, we didn't know what to expect." She said she would talk to her husband, and we left it at that.

Her comment, "We didn't know what to expect," told me a couple of things: 1) Someone advised them, prior to the first night of the program, that Atticus was autistic. Whoever provided that information failed to give any detail of his ability to function in a normal setting, and 2) Instead of talking to Atticus's mother, or other women who have worked with him at the church for years, they automatically assumed he was incapable of participating and keeping up with other children. To God's glory, and to my satisfaction, Atticus proved them wrong in a big way as the year progressed.

I left church that evening sick to my stomach. I couldn't believe Atticus was receiving this treatment inside the church he had been attending for years without any issues up to that point. I couldn't believe they had separated him from the other children, not allowed him to participate in game time, and that I was put in a position where I had to fight this battle at that place. There were times I had to speak up and advocate for my child outside the church setting, but I never thought I would have to do it there.

I was so heartsick over the situation that I decided to contact one of the volunteers who worked with Atticus the previous two years. Since I didn't see what was going on in the lower level of the program, I wanted to make sure they didn't separate him there as well. I was confident they hadn't, but the latest events made me doubt everything I thought I knew.

I sent the volunteer a message and asked her if they separated Atticus from the typical kids in class or at game time. Was he truly incapable of engaging with other children, and I just wasn't told? Her response was, "He was with my group which was regular kids. But Atticus isn't regular, he is awesome."

Her words soothed my soul and made my mission so much more important to carry out.

On the third Wednesday when the director arrived, I left my position at the check-in desk and went straight over to talk to him. I wasn't going to allow anyone or anything to stop me from speaking with him this week.

His wife followed through on her word to talk to him about my concerns. As soon as I told him I needed to speak with him about Atticus, he immediately apologized and continued to apologize several more times throughout our conversation.

He asked me what room color I would like Atticus to go in. I told him

Hello, My Name Is Awesome

Atticus works well with women, so he reassigned Atticus to the red room with a female leader. When game time arrived, not only did Atticus stay and play games, but a couple of other children from the purple room were included as well. As the year progressed, all the children from the purple room were part of game time.

I don't hold any ill will toward the director. I've gone on to serve several more years under his leadership. He's a good, godly man who has spent years serving our Lord and teaching our youth. I have watched him welcome and include many special-needs children since. I tend to believe this was a bitter road I had to travel to sweeten the path for others.

Volunteer to help. Such a strong calling that refused to cease. I tried to ignore it, but in the end, I listened and answered the call.

As the years have passed, it's easy to see that God has always placed people on our path to help Atticus on his journey. From his first speech pathologist to the women of our church, they all accepted Atticus, showed him love, saw his strengths, and encouraged his potential. And when an obstacle was placed before him, God put me there to make sure Atticus would continue to blossom.

***

Journal Entry
May 2012
4 Years 9 Months Old

Today I found clumps of dirt in the chair Atticus sits on. I asked him how the dirt got all over the chair.

Atticus said, "It's Jesus' fault."

I looked at him and asked, "How is it Jesus' fault?"

Atticus answered, "Jesus made the dirt."

***

Journal Entry
August 2012
A Few Days Shy of 5 Years Old

Atticus came home from church a few weeks ago and told me that

Jesus is over 2000 years old.

This was an exciting fact for him to learn because the older someone is the more fascinated he is with the number.

Today, Atticus and I were in the kitchen talking as I prepared lunch. We were discussing what we were going to eat when he changed the topic to Jesus.

He declared, "Christmas is Jesus' birthday!"

I said, "Yes, we celebrate His birthday on December 25th. We can say, 'Happy birthday, baby Jesus!'"

With a serious look in his eyes and a sober tone in his voice, Atticus looked at me and said, "No! Happy birthday, *old* Jesus!"

***

Journal Entry
March 2013
5 Years 7 Months Old

Like many children affected by autism, Atticus has a bit of an obsession with ceiling fans. His dad will feed this obsession by spending their Saturdays together visiting home improvement stores and spending a lot of extra time in the fan section.

Atticus is especially partial to Lowes because they publish a yearly ceiling-fan book he spends hours poring through. The book gives him the knowledge he needs to go into Lowes and tell people all the facts they need to know about a particular ceiling fan—whether they want to know or not.

Atticus just might have the entire ceiling fan section, including the brand, model number, price, and size of each fan memorized. He hasn't been able to find a ceiling-fan book at the other home improvement stores, but he does a pretty good job learning about their fans by visiting the stores often.

After brushing his teeth this evening, it was time for Atticus to say his prayers. He prayed, "Dear Jesus, thank you for this day. Thank you for watching over myself, daddy, and mommy. Please remember our friends, family, and neighbors. Please help my school friends who need help, the people at Lowes who need help, the people at Home Depot who need help, the people at Menards who need help, the people at The Andersons who need

Hello, My Name Is Awesome

help. Amen."

***

Journal Entry
July 2013
5 Years 11 Months Old

A tremendous amount of mother and son interaction takes place in the kitchen. When you're a mom with a little one always under your feet, you can become frustrated and impatient—especially in a small home.

I was trying to prepare a meal. This required me to constantly move back and forth between one counter to another. Every time I made a move, I bumped into Atticus.

I asked him to go sit at the table several times, but he didn't want to leave my area. I finally reached my threshold of patience and sternly said, "Remove thyself."

With contempt in his voice, he looked me directly in the eyes and said, "Why did you say *thyself?* That's a Jesus thing!!!!"

***

Journal Entry
October 2013
6 Years 2 Months Old

For weeks Atticus has heard advertisements on our local Christian radio station that singer Chris Tomlin was coming to town. Every time the announcement was made, Atticus begged me to take him to the concert. Once I found out the tickets didn't cost an arm and a leg, I gave in and took my growing boy to his first concert.

Knowing the loud music would be too much for him to handle, we went prepared with ear protection and expecting to have a great evening. What I didn't expect was his interaction with some of the women attending the event.

Before the concert began, we decided to use the restroom one last time. As we waited, the line grew longer and longer. We were standing in silence when Atticus turned around and addressed all the women in line behind us.

"How many of you trust Jesus?" he asked them.

They all looked down at him. No one said a word as they continued to stare at him, seemingly in disbelief.

Atticus wouldn't be deterred. He asked again—a little louder this time— "How many of you trust Jesus?"

All at once they seemed to understand this child was serious as smiles spread across their faces, and they slowly raised their hands one by one.

***

Journal Entry
December 2013
6 Years 4 Months Old

Last December, when Atticus was five years old, he informed me that he didn't want to visit just one Santa, but he had a goal to, "See a lot of Santas!" I thought this had the potential to be an interesting and fun adventure, so I agreed to join him in his endeavor. My only requirement was we wouldn't visit a Santa that charged us to take a picture.

Throughout our adventure, we discovered there are many locations one can visit Santa for free and take your own picture. We found Santa at such places as the grocery store, the farm market, and restaurants.

One lucky evening, while attending family night at a restaurant, we got a little more than we bargained for when the "real" Santa showed up while one of his "helpers" was getting his picture taken with the kids. Atticus's five-year-old mind reeled. Two Santas at once! That was incredible!

Atticus spent a few minutes chatting with the "real" Santa and eventually asked St. Nick how he got to the restaurant. Santa answered, "A pick-up truck, of course!"

We created several wonderful memories that year and decided to have a similar adventure this year. We're halfway through the Christmas season, and we just wrapped up a visit with yet another Santa.

On the car ride home, with *O Holy Night* playing softly on the radio, I heard a small voice in the back seat say, "Behold, a virgin shall be with child, and shall bring forth a son, and they shall call his name Emmanuel, which being interpreted is, God with us."

     Hello, My Name Is Awesome

Atticus was reading the true Christmas story from the Bible he keeps with him in the car. I was struck how perfect that verse was in that moment. In the midst of our frivolity, God used a six-year-old child to gently remind us why we truly celebrate this time of year.

For me, it was a beautiful, heartwarming God moment that I will forever cherish.

***

Journal Entry
May 2014
6 Years 9 Months Old

We took our weekly trip to Whole Foods today. After we finished shopping, we went to check out. As I was loading the grocery items onto the belt, I heard Atticus begin to talk to the cashier.

"Hello!" he enthusiastically greeted her with a smile and a wave.

Then he asked sincerely, "Do you know Jesus as your Savior?"

The cashier looked at him. She appeared to be a little stunned, as if caught off guard. She remained silent for a few seconds, and Atticus continued to watch her while anticipating her answer. She finally spoke and replied in a quiet voice, "Yes."

With a sparkle in his eyes, Atticus replied, "You do? So do I!"

Oh, how I wish I had this child's boldness.

***

Journal Entry
June 2014
6 Years Old

Atticus just completed his first-ever Vacation Bible School. He had a blast memorizing Bible verses, singing, participating in a game of Let's Make a Deal—where he won a few dollars—and learning more about our Savior through the amazing skits our church pulls off each year.

Atticus had several adult leaders over the group he was in, and one of them was named Elizabeth. Elizabeth just gave birth to a sweet baby boy a few months earlier, and Atticus was excited to hear about the new baby.

During their conversation, Atticus asked what the baby's name was. Elizabeth told him, "Matthew."

Atticus was thrilled to learn this fact and told her, "Oh, that's one of the books in the Bible and one of Jesus' disciples! If you have another baby, you can name him Exodus."

He was serious.

***

Journal Entry
August 2014
A Few Days Shy of 7 Years Old

This afternoon, I was cleaning the kitchen after preparing lunch. Atticus was sitting at the table with his dad while eating a sandwich. I was washing dishes and somehow cut my finger with a knife. I screamed, "Ouch! I cut my finger!"

As I ran water over my damaged digit, I heard Atticus say to his dad, "Let's pray for Mommy."

I turned off the water, looked at them sitting at the table, saw Atticus bow his head, fold his little hands, and begin to pray, "Dear God, we ask that you please heal my mommy's finger. In Jesus' name I pray, Amen."

He raised his head, looked at his dad, and said, "See, I'm a godly man."

It's my prayer that as this child grows, he will always have a heart for God and turn to Him in the good times and the bad. I pray his love for Jesus never grows old and his trust in the Almighty continues to grow and glorify Him as it has so often in Atticus's short life.

***

Journal Entry
September 2014
7 Years 1 Month Old

Atticus has a friend named Samantha whom he's known since birth. When Atticus was six years old, he told me that Samantha would be his wife when they grow up. I find his thoughts amusing, but I gently remind him that future events may not unfold the way he has planned.

While he was preparing for bed tonight, our conversation drifted to the topic of marriage and, of course, that led to who he wants to marry when he grows up.

Atticus said, "I want to get married."

I said, "I'm sure you will."

He said, "I must marry Samantha."

I told him, "Well, I don't know if it will be Samantha. Whoever it is, she must be a good woman."

Atticus responded matter-of-factly, "Well, I won't choose someone like Jezebel who worshipped the fake god Baal!"

***

Journal Entry

July 2015

7 Years 11 Months Old

Independence Day is a special time of year in our home. We celebrate the holiday every year by attending our local parade, cooking out, and watching fireworks in the evening.

Since Atticus has been able to have a conversation, I've always mentioned the Declaration of Independence at this time of year. I never get too involved, limiting our conversation to a few sentences and attempting to answer any questions he may have. Since he likes to talk about such things, certain aspects of the Declaration, the American Revolution, and our founding fathers have been part of several conversations throughout the years.

This evening, as he prayed before going to bed, his words touched my heart, and I believe he's truly beginning to understand why we celebrate this historic day.

His words to our heavenly Father were, "Lord, I just pray that you be with all the people on Independence Day—the day the people in Pennsylvania gave us freedom. It's a special day, Lord. It's about liberty, and you like that."

***

Journal Entry

April 2016
8 Years 8 Months Old

Atticus has had an interest in the solar system from an early age. He's known all the planets since he was four and has memorized many facts about moons, temperatures, and distance.

Tonight, in the middle of his nightly prayer, he said, "…and Lord, thank you for creating the earth. Because if you only created the moon, the sun, and the stars, we wouldn't have a place to live. And please watch over Venus, Jupiter, Mercury, Saturn and all the planets in the solar system."

***

Journal Entry
December 2016
9 Years 4 Months Old

We had just finished eating lunch at Cracker Barrel when our server wished us Merry Christmas. Atticus responded to her by saying, "I have to tell you something. Christmas isn't about opening presents and all that stuff. It's really about the baby Jesus!"

Thank you, Lord, for a child who understands why we celebrate this time of year.

***

Journal Entry
May 2019
11 years old

Today was Grandparents Day at Atticus's school. He doesn't have a grandparent, nor did he have a "special" person to show up for him today, so we were going to leave early and skip the afternoon "celebration." Unfortunately, I found out last minute that he needed to perform during the chapel portion of the event because he's in the 5th grade band. So, we switched gears and planned to leave right after service.

When chapel ended, he had to return his instrument to the music room. Once he put away his baritone, he walked over to his classmate, Lina, who was sitting down locking her clarinet case. Her grandmother was wait-

Hello, My Name Is Awesome

ing patiently nearby. I watched from a short distance as he sat down next to Lina and began to cry. Through his tears, he shared with her the circumstances that left him without anyone except his mom to visit with him today. I had no idea he was feeling so sad. He never shared his feelings with me.

When Lina heard his story, she asked him if he wanted to join her and her grandma. His face brightened as he looked my way and asked if that would be alright. I said yes, and he happily joined his friend and her grandmother for the rest of the day's activities.

The grandmother was warm and welcoming. She listened as Atticus told her about himself and shared his class projects and interests with her. She told others that Atticus adopted her for the day and treated him as kindly as you would expect a grandmother to.

As Atticus and grandma prepared to part ways, he reached out his hand to shake hers. She told him that it was a pleasure meeting him. Then she said, "You're going to do amazing things in this world when you grow up."

I was touched by their kindness—Lina's and her grandma's. She didn't have to share her grandmother with Atticus, but she did so without hesitation. And grandma accepted him without question. They exhibited the true meaning of "love thy neighbor as thyself." They showed him the love of Christ.

Chapter 12
Follow His Lead

Atticus was born with an ear for music. I became aware of his ability to recognize melodies when he began matching them when he was about a year and a half.

He had four toys that played several different melodies and a few of the songs were the same on each toy. He used to collect all the musical toys and put them together in one room. He would begin playing a song on one of the toys, then, as fast as he could, he would find the same song on all the others, until he had all the toys playing the same melody at once. Of course, the music wasn't ever in synch, because he had to push a button to skip random songs in order to get to the song he needed, but he always had the same song playing on every toy before the first one ended.

I don't know if it's typical for kids to recognize melodies so early, but that was my first sign of his musical abilities.

The first three and a half years of his life, Atticus couldn't verbally express to me his love for music, so his matching abilities, and his desire to listen to music by himself for extended periods of time, was all I had to go on. Once he began verbally communicating though, my suspicions proved correct.

Atticus received a child's keyboard when he was two years old. The keyboard came equipped with different songs and musical effects ready to play at the press of a button. He loved to test the assorted buttons and listen to various chimes, bells, horns, and stringed instrument sounds built into the apparatus.

He was four years old when he first displayed an ability to figure out how to play tunes on his own using this inexpensive keyboard. One afternoon I heard the familiar childhood song "Are You Sleeping Brother John" playing. I walked over to where he was sitting, and I realized that the key-

Hello, My Name Is Awesome

board wasn't playing the tune, rather Atticus was playing each note on his own.

I asked him if he was playing the song or if the keyboard was playing the song. He said he was playing it. I asked him how he learned to play the tune, but he didn't have an answer for me. He simply said, "I don't know."

I asked him if he would play it again so I could record him. He complied.

I rushed to find the video recorder before he changed his mind. As I recorded him, he played each note of "Are You Sleeping Brother John" flawlessly. He finished by saying, "I did it again!" He was smiling ear to ear. He was proud of himself, and so was I!

He went on to teach himself "London Bridge is Falling Down" and "Little Drummer Boy."

It soon became clear that he had an amazing ear for music, and his natural talent would require nurturing and support, so I decided that Atticus needed piano lessons.

I struggled for a few months trying to find an instructor I felt comfortable with. I spoke to a couple of piano studios, but I didn't feel they would be a good fit for Atticus. I was given a referral for a private instructor, but the cost was expensive and out of my price range.

After months of searching and nearly giving up, a fellow church member gave me a newspaper clipping with the information of a woman who taught piano out of her home. I took the information, and I called the number a couple of weeks later.

The instructor's name was Mariah. She and I spoke at length over the phone about her experience and Atticus's love for music. During our conversation, I made her aware of his autism diagnosis and the challenges she might encounter. I asked her if she had any experience in that area and if it would be a problem. She advised that she had never taught anyone with autism, but she was willing to try. I felt at ease with her and had a calming peace that she should be the one to give Atticus lessons, and time has proven that feeling correct.

God came through again.

***

As Atticus continued to expand his love of music, he soon became obsessed with orchestras. He spent many weekends watching symphonies on YouTube and conducting the orchestra in the confines of our kitchen.

He spent hours researching the different types of instruments that comprised an orchestra. He provided details about instruments I had never heard of such as the timpani and the bassoon. He drew pictures of instruments and separated each one by its musical family—woodwinds, strings, percussion, and brass.

He dreamed of conducting symphonies around the world. He spent months writing down all the possible combinations of instruments he imagined would make up each of his orchestras. Each desired orchestra would have a different number of instruments from each section, but one thing remained consistent—he would always have the largest orchestra in the history of the world.

After witnessing his newfound love of the orchestra, I decided to surprise him with a trip to see our local symphony perform a Christmas concert when he was seven years old. We sat in the back row, at the very top of the theater, so Atticus was free to conduct as much music as he wished without bothering others in attendance.

He had a great time conducting from his seat, talking to some of the musicians before the show began, speaking with women from the chorus during intermission, and having an impromptu visit with Santa as we were walking out a few minutes early.

Later that month, he took part in a piano recital held at a local church. Several parents and family members of the other students attended.

We sat in the front row. While the other students played, Atticus sat in his seat conducting each piece of music with his arms flailing rhythmically in the air. I'm certain this was distracting for the audience behind us, so I whispered to him several times to calm down, or I gently patted his arm as a signal to stop. Each time I attempted to intervene, he leaned over and loudly whispered, "I'm conducting," then continued to do so. I was unable to stop him.

Hello, My Name Is Awesome

After the recital, we were approached by a woman who introduced herself as Jeanne. She was the mother of one of the students and happened to be the wife of the pastor of the church.

Jeanne told us that she loved Atticus's enthusiasm and spirit throughout the recital and that she is the choir director for the church. She then invited Atticus to join her during choir practice where she would allow him to help conduct the choir. Atticus was overjoyed with the invitation and couldn't wait to take her up on the offer.

Six days later, Atticus attended a choir practice and got to conduct real people for the first time. Jeanne introduced him to the choir members and told them that Atticus would be helping her. He had the charm turned on that evening and shook hands with each person and engaged in conversation with several. He was elated to be there and seemed to be walking on air.

I'm not sure Atticus was supposed to help conduct during the entire practice, but he wasn't budging from the stage. He remained part of the evening from beginning to end apart from a small break somewhere in the middle.

Jeanne was patient with him and showed him the proper way to conduct. Atticus discovered there was a lot more to conducting than just waving your arms around in the air. He was also excited to learn that his piano teacher, who plays piano for the church, had to wait on his signal before she played.

The evening was a blessing to behold. I watched as my seven-year-old autistic son experienced two hours of pure magic. I watched as his dream came to life. I watched as love was poured out on him that evening. I watched as he led prayer when practice was over, and I was reminded that God was working in our lives.

A couple of months later, Atticus stumbled across a program on PBS which featured the Boston Symphony Orchestra. He was captivated by the music bursting out of the speakers. He begged me to record the program for him, and the show became a favorite viewing option for months. He watched it several times per week, and his conducting became more animated as time went on.

One afternoon, I walked downstairs and found him watching the program and conducting in such a way that one would think his arm would remove itself from the socket. The movements were intense but precise. In that moment, I decided to buy him a conductor's baton for his eighth birthday.

Follow his lead. That continues to be my motto.

***

Journal Entry
October 2012
5 Years 2 Months Old

This evening, Atticus's dad told me that Atticus is teaching himself to play "Little Drummer Boy" on his keyboard. I didn't believe him, so I asked Atticus if he could play "Little Drummer Boy" for me so I could record him.

Atticus retrieved his keyboard, sat down in the middle of the living room floor, and began to play.

Sure enough, he was picking out "Little Drummer Boy" note by note. Yes, a couple of the notes were off, but anyone who has ever heard the song could easily recognize what he was playing.

He was a few notes from the end of the song when he began bouncing his knee up and down as he continued to play. Then he blurted out, "I want Bob Segar to give me a call!"

He obviously favors Bob Segar's version of the Christmas classic.

***

Journal Entry
July 2013
5 Years 11 Months Old

Atticus and I met with Mariah earlier this week for his first piano lesson. Upon entering her home, Atticus asked her if she had any ceiling fans in the house. Mariah told him she had one in the dining room and one in the master bedroom.

She led us into the dining room, where the piano sits, and showed Atticus the ceiling fan. He began telling her facts about the fan and asked where she bought it. These things concern him greatly. He then asked to see her ceiling fan in the bedroom. She told him they could look at that fan after

Hello, My Name Is Awesome

the piano lesson.

The lesson went well. Atticus was a bit distracted by the ceiling fan behind him and asked about the bedroom ceiling fan a few times, but Mariah was able to keep things moving, and I think we can call his first piano lesson a success.

Mariah kept her promise and allowed Atticus access to her bedroom to see the ceiling fan after the lesson ended. Atticus found great delight with this fan upon learning it had a remote control, and Mariah gave him permission to use the control to play with the fan's speed for a couple of minutes. I wasn't convinced this was a good idea, as I knew the history of Atticus and ceiling fans, but Mariah was new to this and had no idea the can of worms she opened. I firmly, but gently, ended his ceiling fan fun, and we said our goodbyes and planned to meet again the following week.

The days leading up to his second lesson were a bit trying for me. Atticus didn't want to practice the music she gave him, and the only thing he was excited about was the possibility of playing with Mariah's remote-controlled ceiling fan when he returned for his lesson. He wouldn't stop talking about that ceiling fan.

I finally tried to reason with him. I explained what a great musical talent God had given him and that he shouldn't waste it. I asked him if he liked playing the piano. He said he does.

I told him he would need to practice throughout the week if he wanted to continue with lessons. He told me he wanted to continue with lessons so he could see the remote-controlled ceiling fan. I told him I wasn't paying for lessons just so he could play with a ceiling fan. I reiterated that he would need to practice.

I finally asked, "Do you want to learn how to play the piano or not?"

Atticus replied, "Yes, but I'm not a good instrument player. I'm a good ceiling-fan remoter."

***

Journal Entry
November 2013
6 Years 3 Months Old

Piano lessons have been going well. Mariah has proved to be patient with Atticus and all the questions and somewhat quirky behaviors that accompany him at times. He still gets distracted, and Mariah is usually good at getting him back on track.

He continues to visit the master bedroom to see the remote-controlled ceiling fan on a pretty regular basis, but that has become more of a reward for a successful lesson rather than automatic playtime post lesson.

During today's instruction time, Mariah tried to explain how to play dynamics on the piano. She couldn't get Atticus to play the forte symbol correctly because he was pushing the keys too lightly.

Mariah finally asked, "Can you pretend you're a really big person, like 500 pounds, and you have a lot of weight in your arms, so when you hit the keys, they're really loud?"

Without touching the piano keys, Atticus pointed to the mezzo forte symbol in the book. Mariah explained, "Yes, this one will be a little bit softer."

Atticus replied, "Yeah, like I'm 200 pounds."

"Yes, exactly," Mariah said with a giggle.

He went on to play the dynamics as instructed by his saint of a teacher.

***

Journal Entry
February 2014
6 Years 6 Months Old

We're preparing for Atticus's first visit to the dentist. He will be getting his teeth cleaned, and I am trying to prepare him in advance for what to expect.

Tonight, I explained that he would lay down in a chair; a bright light would shine on his face; and they would use their instruments to scrape the yucky stuff off his teeth.

Atticus's body turned rigid as he began flapping his hands from excitement. He asked, "Can I play their instruments and make lots and lots of music first?!"

"No," I said, disappointing him. "They're not musical instruments—they're dental instruments."

***

Journal Entry
January 2015
7 Years 5 Months Old

We have a local middle school whose mascot is the Jackson Jaguars. Atticus's dad was thrift-store shopping and found a Jackson Jaguars sweatshirt that fit Atticus perfectly, so he bought it for him.

Atticus wore the shirt when he went to work with me today. One of my coworkers, who attended Jackson Middle School, was curious about the sweatshirt he was wearing and asked Atticus, "Who went to Jackson?"

Atticus answered, "Johnny Cash."

Chapter 13
Russell, Party of Three

The Cracker Barrel Old Country Store has been a favorite dining spot of mine for years. I dare anyone to taste the delicious buttermilk biscuits, sawmill gravy, fluffy pecan pancakes with pure maple syrup, or a heaping serving of chicken and dumplings and not walk away a lover of the country style cooking the Cracker Barrel is known for.

When Atticus was three years old, his dad established a weekly boys' night out every Thursday evening, and the Cracker Barrel soon became their main stop for dinner.

In the early days, Tim brought Atticus home each Thursday evening and told me about their dinner and the places they visited afterward. As months flew by, Tim began telling me that the employees at the Cracker Barrel liked Atticus and they let him "help them." I didn't question how Atticus "helped them" because I figured he was just being his normal, delightful self and the Cracker Barrel staff enjoyed his visits.

When Atticus was four years old, Tim walked through the door one evening with a different attitude. He was beaming with pride as he told me the folks at the Cracker Barrel presented Atticus with his very own rising star apron and name tag. I wouldn't have believed it except Atticus was wearing the proof around his neck and waist.

It was then I began to wonder about what went on at the Cracker Barrel. *What actions could result in such a gift?* I concluded it was time to take the Thursday evening happenings at the restaurant a little more seriously and check things out for myself.

The following Saturday I took a trip to the Old Country Store with the guys. I wanted to see exactly what Atticus was doing every Thursday evening that deserved an apron.

Upon entering the doors of the establishment, it was obvious that just about all the workers knew Atticus, and they fawned over him. They greeted him with sweet smiles, pats on the back, and a hug from one of the senior workers.

When employees discovered that I was his mom, they told me how much they adored him, how smart and sweet he was, and what a joy he was to have around. I thought it odd that a little four-year-old boy could have such an impact on a restaurant full of employees.

Atticus made his way over to the host station where more employees promptly greeted him. Before I knew what was happening, a tall, slender, female held his hand and walked with him to seat a group of patrons. When they returned, they escorted the next group in line to their table. It was truly one of the cutest things I have ever witnessed, but I couldn't believe they allowed him to help seat customers.

Atticus continued to help until our table was ready. After we finished our meal, I paid the bill while Atticus and his dad walked toward the doors to go outside. When I met up with them again, they were playing doorman for the customers who were entering and leaving the building.

Atticus welcomed those who were arriving with a hardy, "Welcome to the Cracker Barrel!" To the diners who were leaving he said, "Thank you! Come again!" It was obvious they had engaged in this act many times before, and Atticus was thrilled to be part of it.

A couple of months later, I returned to the Cracker Barrel with them. It was Christmas season and Atticus wore his apron and a Santa hat.

He strutted through the front door with a confidence I could only dream of obtaining. With his head held high, he walked to the host station where he met Shyla. Shyla was one of the regular Thursday evening hosts that allowed Atticus to help her seat people. Atticus's job duties had evidently expanded a bit since my last visit, as he was now asking each person who approached the host station for the number of people in their party.

Things didn't go as smoothly as one would hope at times, however. One group told Atticus that they had four in their party, but Atticus only saw three people standing in front of him. Because Atticus is a literal person, he had to dispute the number of people in the group and replied, "But there are only three of you."

The man speaking for the group told Atticus the other person would join them later. At the same time, a random person walked close to where the conversation was taking place and Atticus said, "Oh, I think this is your fourth person."

The man told Atticus again, "No, the fourth person will be here later."

At that point Shyla stepped in and asked Atticus if he wanted to carry the silverware. Atticus took the silverware, and he and Shyla accompanied the three to their table. Shyla was no longer holding Atticus's hand.

Once Atticus and Shyla returned to the station, we all stood around waiting for more customers to arrive while holiday songs played over the speakers.

Seemingly bored with the lack of work, Atticus spontaneously decided to give the Cracker Barrel employees, and their guests, an unexpected rendition of a holiday classic.

"Jingle Bell Rock" was playing through the overhead speakers. I watched Atticus reach for the intercom mic. He was having trouble, so Shyla unhooked it from the wall and handed it to him. Then she reminded Atticus that he had to push the button on the side so people could hear him when he speaks.

I couldn't figure out why she was handing him the intercom mic when there wasn't a customer to call. It didn't take me long to realize what he was planning though. He placed the mic in front of his mouth, pressed the button, and began to sing. The entire store boomed with the sound of a child's voice singing along to "Jingle Bell Rock."

Atticus belted out the tune on key. He was heard over the recording as he sang into the intercom, smiling and swaying side to side in rhythm with the music. I couldn't help but laugh at the sight while wishing I had a video recorder to capture the moment.

I looked around the room to see the reaction of others in the store. I saw a couple of people shopping, and several people in line waiting to pay for their meals. They were looking around trying to figure out where the child's voice was coming from. They looked at the ceiling first, then began

Hello, My Name Is Awesome

scoping the room—left—then right—craning their necks over clothes racks and candy displays. The ones who were able to see Atticus singing smiled or laughed. The ones who didn't see what was taking place looked confused.

I couldn't believe what I was witnessing. Why did a restaurant allow a four-year-old child to take control of the intercom and sing along with holiday music? I stood in amazement while I saw employees, and a manager, gather around the host station to watch Atticus sing. Their only reaction was to smile.

Once the song ended, Atticus put away the intercom mic. I moved closer to Shyla and told her she probably shouldn't allow Atticus to do things like that. She responded that it took them so long to get him to talk into the intercom that she didn't want to take it from him.

It was clear some of those folks had a great affinity for him.

Atticus and his dad continued their Thursday night Cracker Barrel visits for a couple of years. Eventually, their visits became fewer and farther apart, and most of the employees from their early days left the business with only a handful remaining. Atticus seldom visits that Cracker Barrel location any longer, but when he does, a couple of people still recognize the sweet little boy that used to visit them every Thursday evening.

That location will always hold a special place in my son's memory as it was where his Cracker Barrel fascination began and where total strangers welcomed him as one of their own, offered him encouragement, and showed him extreme kindness.

***

When Atticus was six years old, he and I began a new tradition of visiting the Cracker Barrel most Sundays after church. We visited a different location, on the other side of town, because it was closer to our church.

The first Sunday we walked in the doors of the new location, unfamiliar faces welcomed us. That didn't seem to bother Atticus. He approached the host station as if he was home. Standing tall and smiling, he walked right up to the woman in charge of calling names, read her name tag, and greeted her with a robust, "Hello, Paige!"

And just like that, Atticus rekindled a relationship with the Cracker

Barrel.

He struck up a conversation with Paige about the names on the waitlist that was lying on the podium in front of her. Atticus was interested in how many people were in each party and how long it would take to seat them. His reading skills impressed Paige, and she commented that he was quick to understand the process.

She asked him his name and his age and other questions adults ask kids. I watched in awe as Atticus once again worked his way into the heart of yet another total stranger.

Before our first visit was over, Paige gave Atticus the intercom and allowed him to call names while we waited for our table. But Atticus wouldn't call just any name—it had to be a party of five or more. He wasn't interested otherwise. His love of big numbers prevented him from caring. Paige seemed to find this amusing.

As we developed our new routine, it soon became clear that Paige would be at the host station each Sunday when we arrived, and she always seemed more than happy to see Atticus and allow him to help her. As weeks past, Paige not only allowed Atticus to call names, but she let him stand behind the host podium and mark the names off the list once the party was seated.

Atticus became well-known to many other regular Sunday employees. Each week he was greeted by name and made to feel like he was part of the crew.

As I became more comfortable with the situation, I told Paige that Atticus had a rising star apron that a different Cracker Barrel location gave him when he was four years old. She laughed. I thought she may have believed I was joking, so I told her I wasn't. She said he should wear it on Sundays. So Atticus began wearing his rising star apron every Sunday. People usually smiled and seemed to think this little boy wearing an apron and calling names was adorable.

About a year into our new routine, this Cracker Barrel location went from writing names on paper to a more efficient electronic system for keeping track of groups and seating. Atticus was naturally interested in the new electronic device and didn't have any problem learning the updated proce-

Hello, My Name Is Awesome

dures and the new method of calling names.

Then, we arrived one afternoon to find someone different at the host station. We were told that Paige had been moved to the dining room, but Atticus could still help call names. Paige was within view most of the time from the host station, and Atticus knew the new person calling names, so he didn't have any trouble adjusting to the change.

A major development came out of the shift in positions, however. The new host wanted Atticus to call every party, no matter how small, over the PA system. At first, he resisted. He told her that he only calls parties of five or more, but the new host insisted, so Atticus began calling every name that popped out of the printer.

On certain days, Atticus's interaction with people amazed me. He became excited when large groups arrived and loved to ask them about the number of people in their party and what, if anything, they were celebrating. Over time, I watched as he would high-five groups as they walked into the dining room to be seated. Sometimes he would greet people with a confident and lively "Hello!" as he waved to them or shook their hands. He always caught people off guard and brought a smile to their faces when he interacted with them in such a manner.

Patrons frequently asked him if he was being paid and often complimented him by telling him he was doing a great job. Atticus responded that they don't pay him, but he likes to volunteer on Sundays. On a few occasions, customers have handed him a couple of dollars for a job well done.

While he's working the host station, I stand a few feet away to keep an eye on him. People around us have no idea that I'm his mom, and I often hear them talking about him. They discuss how well he performs the job, how cute he is, and how mature he seems. One day, someone struck up a conversation with me about him. I told her he was my kid. She told me she hopes her boy grows up to be "so together." If only she knew the truth behind his seemingly well-mannered and focused behavior.

Atticus isn't always "so together." There are days I watch him performing his "duties" at the Cracker Barrel, and I need to remind him to pay attention to people who are talking to him. He tends to interact on his terms only. Oftentimes customers are interested in talking to him when he is behind the host podium, and Atticus gets too distracted by other things that are going on and doesn't respond to some inquiries. I feel it necessary to try to reinforce positive interaction with him whenever I witness this happening.

After a couple of years of helping most Sundays, a manager at his newest Cracker Barrel home presented Atticus with a new apron. He retired his rising star and began wearing a crisp, clean, four-star apron with his name embroidered on the front. He was so excited when he saw it the first time that his eyes lit up brighter than Christmas morning. His response to the new apron was, "They skipped the first-, second-, and third-star apron." I told him they must think he's a really great worker.

As of this writing, Atticus continues to help call names most Sundays at the Cracker Barrel. He loves to perform his "job" and mingle with the staff. He talks often of growing up and becoming a real employee and working the host station on his own when he's sixteen.

I don't know what the future holds, or the plans the Lord may have for him, but I'm prayerful that Atticus will continue to bless hearts and touch lives wherever he goes.

I'm thankful for people like Paige and the other employees at Cracker Barrel who have played a role in my son's overall growth and development by allowing him the freedom to be himself and take part in a task that he truly enjoys. He's been given real-world experiences with people and situations that he otherwise wouldn't have received.

I believe his Cracker Barrel encounters have helped in his overall social, language, and behavioral development and has forced him outside of his comfort zone on more than one occasion. As I have learned, that usually ends up being a good thing.

***

Journal Entry
January 2013
5 Years 5 Months Old

My mother passed away sixteen months ago. Since then, Atticus has reminded me daily of my loss. He will blurt out, for no apparent reason, things like, "Oh, your mom is dead," or, "I'm so sad my grandma isn't alive. I

Hello, My Name Is Awesome

wish my grandma was here. My grandma loved me so much."

Every time we drive through the city where she passed, Atticus feels the need to remind me, "Your mom died here."

He's unrelenting, and no matter how much I try to reason with him and ask him to stop, he continues. I understand this behavior is all part of his obsessive nature, but that knowledge doesn't make those moments any less painful.

Atticus recently began asking both strangers and acquaintances, "Is your mom alive?" I told him not to ask people that question. We often discussed why that question might make them sad if their mom is no longer with them. He eventually stopped asking that particular question, but he continues to be obsessed with how old a person is.

This afternoon, Atticus and I went to Cracker Barrel for lunch. Before we went inside, I told him he wouldn't be helping the host today because we were only there to eat. He was fine with that.

There wasn't a large crowd, so we were seated immediately.

Our waitress came to our table and said hello to Atticus. She knew him from his many visits with his dad on Thursday evenings. We both said hello to her, but before she could say anything else, Atticus asked, "How old is your mom?"

The waitress looked at him, paused, took a deep breath, and said, "She was sixty-two."

My immediate thought was, *Oh, no! She said was.*

I couldn't recover fast enough.

Atticus said, "But how old *is* she?"

The waitress said again, "She was sixty-two."

Before I could speak his name, Atticus said louder, "But how old *IS* she?"

The woman's eyes filled with tears.

I said, "Atticus, stop. She already told you. Stop." I shot him the mom look.

Atticus stopped talking, and the waitress turned to me and told me her mom died four months ago. I told her I was sorry and that I understood how hard it is because I lost my mom a year ago. Both the waitress and I were crying. Emotion overcame us, and we began hugging in the middle of the dining room. When we finished comforting each other, I told her to take a break and not to worry about us. She could come back when she was ready.

After she left the table, I had another talk with Atticus about asking people about their mom. I tried to make him understand how upset our waitress was because of that simple question, and the way he refused to let it drop. He must have understood, because he didn't say anything else to the waitress about her mom, but each time she came back to our table, her eyes were puffy and sad, her lips drawn down. She attempted to smile but the pain was evident and real. I could tell she was crying in between trips and just trying to keep her composure while serving us.

This was just one of many uncomfortable moments I've experienced with a child who obsesses and can't let anything go.

***

Journal Entry
November 2014
7 Years 3 Months Old

When tending the host station, Atticus will occasionally run across a name that he's not sure how to pronounce and will ask for help. Today, the name *Talbot* was on the wait-list. This is not a spelling that would normally stump him, but when he announced, "Tall-butt, party of six, your table is now available," I almost died of embarrassment and laughter.

Surely this will end his Cracker Barrel career.

The host's face was red as she unsuccessfully tried to stifle her amusement. I was trying to calm my hilarity by taking deep breaths while my mind bristled with fear that the family might show up angry.

A couple of minutes passed when a group approached the host station. They were all grinning. The woman leading her family smiled at Atticus and said, "The Tall-butts are here!" Everyone within earshot burst out laughing. I breathed a sigh of relief that she played along with the mispronunciation of her name.

It seems Atticus's job is safe—for now.

***

    Hello, My Name Is Awesome

Journal Entry
December 2015
8 Years 4 Months Old

Atticus had an excellent day interacting with Cracker Barrel customers as they waited for their tables—shaking hands, high-fiving, explaining the daily special, and telling them that he usually calls large groups but today he's calling small groups as well.

When it was our turn to be seated, we went to our table and placed our order. While we were eating, a woman came over to our table, handed Atticus a folded napkin, and told him, "This is for you." Then she left.

Thank You was written on the outside. We opened the napkin and found a note and a five-dollar bill inside. The note read:

> Young Man,
> Your kindness and youth has brought the true meaning
> of Christmas Spirit to our hearts. Never stop warming
> other's hearts with your good deeds, as it pays off in
> many ways.
> Thank you for making us smile.
> The Russell party of 3

***

Journal Entry
April 2016
8 Years 8 Months Old

While Atticus was calling names today at Cracker Barrel, one of the managers asked me if she could take a picture of him "working" to put in the company newsletter. I gave her my permission, and she proceeded to snap a couple of photos of him.

After we took our seats, I passed this information to our friend, Delilah, who joined us for lunch. She looked at Atticus and said, "Wow! You're very important!"

Atticus replied, "I'm not that important. I didn't ask to be a world-famous star."

He's famous at Cracker Barrel anyway.

***

Lunchtime at Cracker Barrel was unusually busy today. At times the waiting area was so cramped you couldn't take a step without bumping into someone. As is customary, I took my place to the left of the host station, so I could keep an eye on Atticus as he called names.

All the people milling around distracted me, and I took my eyes off the host station for a couple of minutes. When I returned my attention to that area, I found Atticus alone with no employee in sight.

I asked him where the employee went, and he told me she had to use the restroom.

I stepped back and watched as he tried to keep things moving on his own, but I was annoyed that the employee left an eight-year-old child by himself to handle the name-calling duties. There was a lot more required of this job than simply calling names, and I wasn't certain Atticus was up to the challenge.

I watched while he called each name when the ticket popped out of the printer. Once the party made their way to the station, Atticus talked aloud to himself about what he had to do in order to get them seated.

Since he was alone, he not only had to keep track of the names he called, but he also had to retrieve the flatware, and any required kid's menus, then hand those items, plus the ticket, to the runner who was waiting to seat the patrons. This is a multi-step process that Atticus will naturally have problems with, so he had to talk himself through each step in order to accomplish the task.

For example, Atticus would call a party— "Smith party of four, your table is now available." When the family arrived at the host station, Atticus asked them their name. When he discovered they were a party of four, he began talking to himself: "Okay. Smith party of four. I need to get four silverware. One, two, three, four. Now I need menus. I have to give the ticket to her. Do you need any kid's menus? I need one kid's menu…" This one-person dialogue would continue with each new party. Because Atticus was literally thinking out loud, any thought he had in between each step was also spoken.

During the process of working his new responsibilities, Atticus called two older women, who appeared to be in their late sixties, to the host station. They watched as Atticus took care of the group in front of them. When it was their turn, Atticus began the process again, speaking each step aloud. As he was turning to reach for the flatware, one of the senior women touched his arm, leaned close to his face, and said, "You talk too much. You know that?"

I was immediately hurt for my boy and appalled at the heartless words this woman spoke. If she only knew the struggles this child has gone through in his short life. If she only knew what a miracle it was that he was standing there able to do this job—even if he did have an unorthodox way of going about it—would she be so cruel?

Atticus looked at her for a split second. Then he turned his back to her, looked at the wall, and with elbows bent and hands firmly in front of his face, he said, "I don't need a grandma messing around with me and telling me I talk too much, because I don't!" He then continued to talk his way through getting her flatware and handing the utensils to the person seating them.

When the host returned from the restroom, Atticus was able to relax and take a breath. That's when he looked at me and said, "She told me I talk too much!"

I could tell her words hurt him. I told him I heard what she said and not to let it bother him.

The truth is, he does talk a lot. At times, his constant ramblings can be overwhelming. But this is a child who I thought at one point would never talk, so I try to always be thankful for his ability to speak rather than discourage him from doing so.

He rarely takes a breather unless he's in a classroom setting or church. He simply has an overwhelming desire to talk. But there are times when he's not talking just to be talking. Such was the case at Cracker Barrel this day. He had to talk himself through a multi-step process so he could perform the job at hand.

I'm confident he was anxious and a bit nervous, although he said otherwise. When he had to do the job by himself, his entire body language changed. He became rigid and stiffer with each movement. His fingers moved rapidly up and down. At times, the thumbs and middle fingers met in a repetitive, tapping motion—a stimming behavior he engages in when overwhelmed. He isn't even aware it is happening.

Even so, he stepped up and met the challenge presented to him. While I was annoyed with the worker for leaving him alone and the callous remark of one of the patrons, I was thankful God gave him the ability to handle the pressure.

***

Journal Entry
July 2016
8 Years 11 Months Old

Our trip to Cracker Barrel began as any other today. As we pulled into the parking lot, Atticus was excited to help call names and interact with the employees and customers. Before we entered the building, he put on his brand-new, four-star apron, and confidently walked through the doors and up to the host station.

I lagged a little behind, but once I arrived near the host station, Atticus looked my way and waved me over. He looked like he was going to cry.

I walked to his side, and he whispered in my ear that the host didn't want him to help. I wasn't sure what was going on. She wasn't a new employee, and she has known Atticus for a while. There were not many customers, so it wasn't busy. I told Atticus to stay with me, and within five minutes, we were seated.

Once we were at our table, we discussed calling names at the host desk. Atticus was upset that he was told he couldn't help today. I understood that he was upset, because calling names every Sunday has been his routine for years, so he expects to be able to participate each time he arrives.

I tried to explain that the host must be having a bad day, and we needed to be aware that sometimes people can be a little overwhelmed and not want to be bothered. My words, coupled with not being allowed to help at the host station, were interpreted by Atticus to mean that he was never going

Hello, My Name Is Awesome

to be able to call names at Cracker Barrel again. His eyes filled with tears as his lips trembled. He was visibly upset.

Paige happened to look over in our area at the time he was crying, and she came over to our table. She asked him what was wrong. Atticus told her he wasn't allowed to call names, and he will never be able to call names again.

She apologized and told him that he will definitely be able to call names in the future. Atticus took Paige's words as a promise and was able to calm down a bit.

A few minutes later, a manager came to our table. The manager asked Atticus how he was doing. Atticus struggled to use his words, but eventually said, "I'm fine now that every problem has been solved, and, and, and every, and every deal has been made."

The manager looked at me for an answer.

I said, "He's fine."

The manager then told Atticus, "Good! We'll get you up there calling names next week. Okay?"

Atticus said, "Okay."

Atticus didn't have to wait until next week. While we were eating, Paige came over to Atticus and told him she needed his help to call a party of fourteen. She brought joy to his heart in that moment. He sprang out of his chair and followed her to the host station to call the party of fourteen. He returned to our table with the biggest smile on his face. A few minutes later Paige needed his help to call a party of twelve.

As we were leaving, I stopped to thank Paige for her kindness. She told me how much she loves Atticus and that she considers him part of their Cracker Barrel family. Her affection for him warmed my heart.

Faces change regularly at Cracker Barrel. This experience taught us that Atticus may not always be able to work the host station, as new names and faces appear often. Still, there was a blessing in the middle of this lesson. I was reminded once again of God's love for Atticus, and I praised Him for placing loving people like Paige in my child's life.

***

Journal Entry

January 2017

9 Years 5 Months Old

Atticus was working the host station today at Cracker Barrel when a woman came up to the podium wearing an OSU shirt. Atticus told her he likes Michigan, but since Jake Butt is graduating, he's going to root for OSU now.

Then he began chatting with the woman about OSU's recent bowl loss by saying, "Man, they had a disappointing loss!"

The woman said, "They've had a lot of disappointing losses, but that one hurt so bad I couldn't even speak. They just didn't show up that day!"

Atticus replied, "They did show up. They just didn't play well."

Chapter 14
Mommy Loves Me in the Evening, Under the Moon.

I recently saw an Internet meme that declared: "My Son has the Kind of Autism No One Talks About." I immediately knew the meme represented parents of children with a severe form of autism.

As I perused the comment section of the post, I read each mother's confession of how exhausting it is to have a non-verbal child, a violent child, a sleep-challenged child, a screaming child, and a child who plays with feces. I read comments from real mothers struggling with what feels like a hopeless situation.

Most seemed exhausted and worn out by all they endure on a daily basis. Unfortunately, most of them also seemed to have a common contempt for the label *autism* being used to diagnose children with the ability to function at a higher level—you know, the kind of autism people *do* talk about.

The autistic quirky kid. The autistic smart kid. The autistic basketball player. The autistic teenager who scored a date to the prom. The autistic child who seems to function just fine to the outside world because he can walk, talk, and socialize to some extent.

One commenter argued these children don't have "real autism," and several others agreed. As I read their discussions, I couldn't believe how they were diminishing the trials and anguish of families affected by a form of autism outside of their norm. Not only that, but they were also unwittingly belittling the severe struggles that each of the children on the higher end of the spectrum endure on a personal level.

I'm here to tell those mothers that these kids battle every day of their lives. Their families are affected in ways they never saw coming, and the world of so-called high-functioning autism isn't a walk in the park on a perfect autumn morning.

As I continued to read the Internet conversations, my thoughts reflected on an evening Atticus and I spent with another mother and her autistic child a few years earlier.

In those days, I was still struggling with the diagnosis Atticus had received just a few months prior. During my discussions with the therapist, she made a point of telling me she was diagnosing Atticus with autism, not Asperger's syndrome, and she explained the difference. At the time, they considered Asperger's syndrome a separate diagnosis.

As the mother and I watched Atticus interact with others in our surroundings and explore his environment, she seemed dismayed that Atticus received an autism diagnosis and commented that she thought he should have been diagnosed with Asperger's syndrome instead. I didn't let her know, but her comment stung and angered me. How dare she judge him after knowing him for an hour!

She didn't live with Atticus the previous four years of his life. She didn't witness the obstacles he worked so hard to overcome. She didn't witness the countless hours of speech therapy, occupational therapy, and physical therapy he endured. She never witnessed *this* exhausted mother leading the effort to equip my child with the skills and the ability to function in our society as he grows, or the countless hours I spent pleading with him to produce a single syllable.

She never witnessed his struggle or inability to do simple things we take for granted every day. She wasn't aware of his feeble attempts to cross his midline, or his inability to use scissors or ride a tricycle. She knew nothing of his weak muscle tone or his attempts to perform a wheelbarrow walk—only to fail miserably—because he was too weak to hold himself up longer than a couple of seconds, or how he struggled to alternate his hands—left, right, left, right! She never witnessed the silence in our home.

She didn't know he couldn't follow an object with only his eyes but used his entire head instead. She never witnessed his meltdowns or irrational thought patterns that lead to irrational fears and behaviors that are unstoppable. She didn't see his struggle to process thoughts or produce words

Hello, My Name Is Awesome

to verbalize a problem or need.

She was blissfully unaware how his affliction impacted our lives.

How could I expect her to understand when even friends and family didn't know or understand? All anyone knew about Atticus was that he was a smart, talkative, and friendly four-year-old child, because that's all most people outside of our home ever witnessed.

But she certainly felt she knew all she needed to know to diagnose my child and put him in the correctly labelled box—the box she felt he belonged in. And why not? She obviously judged autism by her own experience and concluded, much like the commenters on the Internet, that Atticus didn't have "real" autism.

So, I continued to read the comments, and I continued to think of that mom. My thoughts resolved that mothers like myself struggle as much as mothers like them. Only they don't realize we have so much in common because our struggles are different.

It's often been said that "If you've met one person with autism, you've met one person with autism." I love this quote because it's accurate. There may be many common themes, but no one person is the same, I believe it would serve everyone in the autism community well if we respected the challenges present in the lives of all families affected by autism—no matter the severity.

Atticus struggles with more issues than I'm writing about in this book. If I tried to delve deeper into each one of them, I couldn't develop an ending. I've tried to maintain a positive tone and focus mainly on his achievements and victories, but there are many more obstacles to overcome.

Adults see Atticus as smart, kind, and able to take care of himself. They are unaware that he continues to struggle with self-care and personal hygiene. They don't have to worry that he can't independently walk down the street or through a parking lot because he has no sense of danger and is unable to navigate either situation visually or mentally.

They don't realize that Atticus can't read body language, and he misinterprets emotions and voice tones, leading to misunderstandings and meltdowns that spiral out of control. He is unable to self-regulate his emotions during those situations. If you don't understand Atticus, and very few who know him understand him, you will think he's being dramatic or over the top, when he's only responding to how he interprets the situation, which is very different than you or me.

People are unaware of his sensitivity to touch and how he will misinterpret a tap on the shoulder as abuse, or his dislike of open-ended questions that he struggles to answer and usually develops into confusion and a screaming session of "I don't know!"

Atticus can function in a classroom setting, but it comes at a mental, emotional, and physical cost. I've observed him, and his body language is rigid, his facial expression tense. He doesn't assert himself in many schoolroom situations, and he is terrified that he will make the teacher angry if he doesn't follow every rule to a T.

Anxiety builds throughout his school day. He strangles his energy to focus on keeping calm and holding himself together throughout the day. When evening comes, his mom is left to deal with the inevitable emotional and physical explosion that results.

Incessant talking is our evening norm. Atticus simply must talk, and the topic is always of his choosing, which is usually his current obsession. When I remove myself from the conversation, he will script books, game shows, sporting events, or YouTube videos.

He literally runs through the house, releasing pent-up energy. Try as I might, I've been unsuccessful in my attempts to stop him from running on the couch and jumping on the chair. He'll stand on his head, practice forward rolls, skip from room to room, while talking the entire time.

Occasionally, the release will come in the form of severe stimming—flapping, spinning, and sudden, body-jolting, vocal outbursts that neither form words nor have meaning. He'll experience meltdowns over something as simple as having to do a one-page math sheet for homework, performing a chore he's responsible for, or taking a shower.

When I use the term *meltdown*, I don't mean he's throwing a fit. He stopped that practice when he was three years old because he realized after the first one that I didn't play those games. No, a meltdown is uncontrollable emotion that, in Atticus's case, results in uncontrollable crying and a sense that the world is caving in on him.

He will cry irrationally, sometimes while running nonsensically around the room, and he can't control his emotion. It's impossible, and he needs help coming out of that dark, upsetting place. Suggestions to, "Stop crying," or "Calm down," don't help Atticus—they only intensify his emotion. He feels misunderstood and alone.

Through the years, I've found if I verbalize his pain, rub his back, and hug him, he will begin to find some comfort. However, it may take more than an hour—and sometimes a few hours—to resolve his meltdown before we achieve some sense of normalcy.

The past few years have been quite the journey complete with unforeseen struggles and an unexpected education—all amid an extraordinary adventure:

- The struggle to understand a child who functions so differently than I anticipated, learning what triggers his anxiety and stress and then figuring out how to help him find calm in the midst of his storms.
- The struggle to adjust to his world of limited thought processes and learning how to help him through the moments when he can't explain why he is feeling sadness or pain.
- The struggle to balance his negative behaviors with real-world discipline that doesn't impede his ability to grow and learn.
- The struggle to watch as friends don't understand the way he thinks, feels, and processes situations differently than they do and the incredulous looks on their faces as I try to explain something they obviously will never understand.
- The ups and downs—the victories and defeats.

It's not over yet. We have a lifetime ahead of us, and if the Lord allows, we'll continue to navigate this journey together.

I have no idea what the future holds for my precious Atticus. I only know that I pray daily for him, and I ask God to continue to provide for him—provide hope, provide friendship, provide companionship, provide independence.

At this point, Atticus's future is uncertain. Will he be able to live an independent life? If not, who will be there to protect him and help him? Who will be there to understand his needs and help him cope with uncomfortable, unhappy, and hurtful circumstances? Who will know how to calm him and talk him through his irrational thoughts and emotions? Who will love him and show him mercy and grace like his mommy? There isn't another living soul who understands him the way I do, and no one who can take care of him as well as I can.

As his mother, I stand in fear at times when I contemplate his future. As with all mothers of special-needs children, I pray I will live as long as he does. For if death comes, who will take care of my child? In those moments, I must step back and remember to whom Atticus truly belongs. I have put my son's life in God's hands. He has been generous thus far.

Atticus has overcome many obstacles in his young life, but there are many more to overcome. I have faith that God will continue to allow Atticus the ability to grow and accomplish great things in this life. We just have to rely on the fruit of the spirit that Atticus spoke so eloquently about in his first-grade chapel performance—*patience*.

"Patience—it also means to be patient for answers to prayers that might take years to be answered."

***

Journal Entry
January 2011
3 Years 5 Months Old

Atticus has been fighting a head cold lately. This afternoon his nose was especially runny, so I sat him on the counter and attempted to clear his nasal passage. As I was wiping his nose I asked, "Where did all this snot come from?"

Atticus happily answered, "Michigan!"

***

Journal Entry
July 2011
3 Years 11 Months Old

Hello, My Name Is Awesome

We experienced a night of heavy rainfall. On the way to church this morning, we drove past the dog park, which flooded from the downpour.

My mind was startled at the sight of water standing fence high, and I shouted, "Wow! Look at all the water! The dog park is under water!"

Atticus said, "It's for ducks now!"

***

Journal Entry
August 2011
A Few Days Shy of 4 Years Old

Atticus has a nasty habit of deliberately saying something different, or the opposite, of what is true. For example, if the word is *slow* he will say *fast*, or if he counts twelve items, he will tell you there's one hundred items. He thinks this behavior is hilarious, and an added bonus is he knows it drives mommy crazy, so he continues with glee.

I always tell him that when he starts school, if he answers questions wrong, the teacher will mark it with an X, and he will fail the class.

Today, I was driving down the road with Atticus in the back seat. We make this trip several times a week when I drop him off at his dad's work. Because Atticus is obsessed with street signs, he knows the name of every cross street as we head north.

Today, he decided that he didn't want to say the actual name of the roads, so Welch Avenue became, "We EVER." Barthman Avenue became, "Bathroom EVER."

With each road we passed the behavior continued.

When we arrived near the end of the road, Atticus stopped changing street names and exclaimed, "They will mark it with an X!"

I said, "Yes, they will mark it with an X because it's wrong."

Atticus said, "X is my new favorite letter!"

***

Journal Entry
September 2011
4 Years 1 Month Old

I picked up Atticus from school today. On the way home he said, "I have to pee!"

"Can you wait until we get home?" I asked.

"Yes," he said.

We arrived home without incident. As I was exiting the car, I said, "Hurry, let's get inside and go potty."

I ran to the door, put the key in the lock, then realized Atticus wasn't with me. I turned around, and there he stood—in the driveway, pants down to his ankles, peeing in the rain.

***

Journal Entry

November 2011

4 Years 3 Months Old

As I was putting Atticus to bed tonight, he said, "Mommy loves me in the evening, under the moon."

I do. I really do. And every other minute of the day as well.

***

Journal Entry

November 2012

5 Years 3 Months Old

I've read that children affected by autism seem to be distant emotionally when it comes to dealing with or understanding the death of a loved one. I'm not sure if that's entirely true, but I know my experience with Atticus tends to make me a believer. Or, perhaps, talking incessantly about the death of someone is just his way of coping with the loss.

Whatever the case may be, Atticus never fails to find an opportunity to bring up the loss of my mother. He isn't trying to be mean, but the constant reminders of my mother's death overwhelm me emotionally at times.

I'm a fan of the Michigan Wolverines football team. Yes, the team has seen rough times in recent years, and they lost another game today, but I continue to cheer for them.

While I was making supper, I said to Atticus, "Michigan lost today and that makes me sad."

Using his most sympathetic voice, Atticus said, "Awww, that's not good." Then he deadpanned, "And your mom is dead too. And your grandma."

Salt, meet wound.

***

Journal Entry
January 2013
5 Years 5 Months Old

Overwhelmed by life today, I said, "I have a busy life."

Atticus questioned, "You have a dizzy wife?"

The light-hearted exchange reminded me of the annoying, and often wrong, auto-correct feature on mobile devices and gave me a brief respite from the burdens of life.

***

Journal Entry
March 2013
5 Years 7 Months Old

Atticus was in the basement playing with his trains when I called him up for breakfast this morning. He responded by standing at the bottom of the stairs and yelling, "You are a mean mother! I am so sick and tired of you! I wish I had a different mother! You are being very mean!"

I calmly replied, "Get up here and eat breakfast anyway."

***

Journal Entry
September 2013
6 Years 1 Month Old

Atticus and I were sitting at Whole Foods, enjoying our weekly lunch date, when a little boy and his grandma walked by us. Atticus looked at the boy, waved, and excitedly said, "Hi, awesome!"

The little boy, and his grandma, gave Atticus a weird look as they continued to walk by. Atticus then looked at me and said, "His shirt says, 'Hello, my name is Awesome.'"

***

Journal Entry
November 2013
6 Years 3 Months Old

When I remember the days my child never spoke a word, simple moments like tonight fill me with gratitude I can't adequately express.

After I tucked him into bed, I was closing his bedroom door, and he said, "Remember I love you."

I will always remember, my beautiful boy, and I will always be thankful you can speak those words.

***

Journal Entry
December 2013
6 Years 4 Months Old

Atticus usually isn't too specific with gifts he wants for Christmas. This year, however, contrasts dramatically with years past. As early as October, he has been asking for a tuba—a real, life-sized, thirty-pound tuba. I'm not sure where the fascination with tubas came from except that he loves orchestras.

He also discovered what an iPad is this year and decided he wants one of those as well. Then, in the typical Atticus fashion I've come to enjoy, he requested a belt for his pants.

Today, he went to visit Santa Claus. While sitting on Santa's lap, Atticus told him exactly what he wants for Christmas. "Well, the first thing I want is a tuba. The second thing I want is called an iPad. The third thing I want is a belt."

Santa was taken aback by the tuba request and told Atticus a tuba is an awfully large instrument for such a small child, but Atticus was adamant.

After they discussed the Christmas list and had their picture taken, Atticus visited with the elves for a few minutes while we waited on our picture.

When we were ready to leave, Atticus had to speak to old Saint Nick one last time. He ran back up to Santa and cheerfully reminded him to, "See what you can do about that tuba!"

***

Journal Entry
April 2014
6 Years 8 Months Old

Atticus got into trouble today. Consequently, he wasn't allowed to play with his Kindle. He decided to try to make me feel bad, so he said, "You are the worst mother in the world!"

I simply replied, "You're welcome."

***

Journal Entry
April 2014
6 Years 8 Months Old

In a social game at school today, Atticus's teacher asked him the question, "When does my mom get angry?"

Atticus answered, "My mom gets angry when I make bad choices. My mom also gets angry when my dad makes bad choices."

***

Journal Entry
May 2014
6 Years 9 Months Old

Atticus called me stupid today. I decided to dole out some old-school punishment and made him write, "I will not call my mother stupid," twenty times. He wasn't happy with the consequence, but he complied.

As he was writing the sentences, I heard him say, "Stupid is not your name. Your name is mommy and that's the truth. I'm sorry to call you stupid, but sometimes it just happens!"

***

Journal Entry
June 2014

6 Years 10 Months Old

We were eating lunch at the Olive Garden today when Atticus said, "I don't like this broccoli. It doesn't have your love in it."

***

Journal Entry
August 2014
7 Years Old

I dropped Atticus off at school this morning. I said, "Have fun, and remember I love you."

He replied, "I always remember that."

***

Journal Entry
October 2014
7 Years 2 Months Old

We went to Dominoes to pick up a pizza this evening. While we were waiting at the counter, Atticus began jumping around and trying to ask the cashier a question. Unfortunately, he couldn't say anything except, "but…but…but…"

I finally said, "What do you need? Just say it!"

He asked her, "Where is the closest bathroom?"

He had urgency in his voice, and I could see now that he clearly had to go. The cashier looked at him, then looked at me, but she didn't answer his question.

I paid the bill while Atticus continued to engage in the pee dance.

The cashier looked for our order and then returned to tell us it wasn't ready yet.

Atticus asked her again, "Where is the closest bathroom?"

She once again looked at him, then looked at me, without saying a word.

I decided to take charge and told him there wasn't a bathroom he could use and took him outside.

We reached our car, and I told him to get in the back seat. I found a used water bottle on the floorboard and told him to pee in the bottle. I made sure he kept his shirt down in case someone drove up beside us. He relieved himself in the bottle and a look of pure happiness swept across his face.

We hopped out of the car and headed back inside the crowded Dominoes. As soon as we entered the door, Atticus lifted both hands in victory and loudly announced, "WE USED A WATER BOTTLE!"

***

Journal Entry
November 2014
7 Years 3 Months

A boy in Sunday school upset Atticus today. He was screaming in Atticus's face and disrupting the entire class.

Atticus came to me after Sunday school and told me he was sick. I asked him what happened, and he told me the boy upset him and the teachers wouldn't let him come to me. He also said he couldn't go to church now because he is sick, and he needs to be with me.

I went to the classroom to talk to the teachers who verified all that Atticus told me. They said one of the other children, Jill, gave Atticus a hug and tried to calm him down. I thought that was kind but told them if anything like that happens again, they need to bring Atticus to me immediately. They said they would.

Atticus continued to complain that he was too sick to go to church and he needed to be with me. I told him, "Jill gave you a hug to try to calm you down and make you feel better."

"Yes," he said, "but it didn't work."

I said, "Maybe not, but it was really nice of her."

Atticus said, "Yes, but it didn't matter. I needed your love. Your love is the best love."

***

Journal Entry
November 2014
7 Years 3 Months

I volunteer as a teacher's assistant in the Sunday school department at our church. Last weekend our superintendent, Mr. Arnold, announced in front of all the children that there is a meeting for all the teachers and assistants next Sunday morning at 9:15. He then said that every person needed to be present, or he would "throw you in the pond."

Maybe not the most appropriate thing to say in front of a bunch of 6-, 7-, and 8-year-old children, but we all knew he was kidding.

Well, "next Sunday" is here, so I woke Atticus up and put him in the shower. I told him he needed to hurry. He asked why, and I told him I had a meeting at church.

His eyes grew wide, and his body began to shake. He stuttered, "Oh, no! Oh, no!"

I could see tears forming in his eyes and panic taking control of his body. "What's wrong?" I asked.

Atticus struggled to explain, "I have to hurry! We need to get you to church, or Mr. Arnold will throw you in the pond! Oh, no!"

I tried to calm his fears, which was no easy task. I told him Mr. Arnold was only kidding, and he wasn't going to throw anyone in a pond. I reassured him over and over that everything would be all right, and he eventually believed me—I think.

I felt terrible that he suffered such fear with the belief that someone was going to throw his mother in a pond, but at the same time, I felt happy that he cared.

***

Journal Entry
December 2014
7 Years 4 Months

Atticus lost a tooth last night. While we were getting ready to brush his teeth this morning, he asked, "Did the tooth fairy come last night?"

I'm certain my face had a look of panic on it as I frantically tried to figure out how to get a dollar under his pillow while standing in the bathroom with him.

I looked at my sweet boy and said, "Oh." I had nothing else.

Atticus began crying and yelled in a hurt, childish voice, "YOU FOR-GOT, DIDN'T YOU??!!!"

Yes. Yes, I did.

Now I had to do damage control and hope it would work. I told him, "It's okay! It's okay! We'll recreate it! It'll be fun!"

I told him to go back to bed. I turned off the lights, closed the door, and ran downstairs to grab two dollars. I mean, two dollars is the least I could do for being such a loser tooth fairy.

I went back upstairs and found Atticus playing his part perfectly, lying in bed and pretending to be asleep. I slipped two dollars under his pillow and closed the door as I left the room.

I waited a minute then knocked and said, "Atticus, it's time to get up."

He jumped up, smiling. I asked, "Did the tooth fairy come last night?"

He looked under his pillow, found two dollars, and restarted the day with a smile on his face. Then he asked, "Does the tooth fairy live in a castle made of teeth?"

***

Journal Entry
January 2015
7 Years 5 Months

I had to discipline Atticus again today. While sitting in timeout he said, "I am Atticus. I came here not to be punished, but since you did that, I am not going to love you anymore."

I know he doesn't mean it, so I find it charming and write about it.

***

January 2015
Journal Entry
7 Years 5 Months

While lying in bed, after saying his prayers, Atticus said, "Mommy, I love God. He gave me a wonderful life and a wonderful mother."

I told you he didn't mean those ugly words he spoke earlier.

***

Journal Entry

March 2015

7 Years 7 Months

Since Atticus began talking, he hasn't stopped. Sometimes I feel overpowered by the constant barrage of words and just need a break. I try not to say anything to him about it, but today I reached a breaking point. I just needed a moment of peace and exclaimed, "Please stop talking for just one minute!"

Without hesitation, Atticus replied, "I have to talk to live."

***

Journal Entry

June 2015

7 Years 10 Months

As I was putting him to bed this evening, Atticus said, "Stay by my side always."

***

Journal Entry

June 2015

7 Years 10 Months

I was hungry this afternoon and told Atticus I was thinking about going to Chipotle.

He said, "You're overweight. You don't need to go to Chipotle."

I told him he shouldn't say things like that to people.

He replied, "But it's more polite than saying you're fat."

***

Journal Entry

March 2016

8 Years 7 Months

While watching the Brain Game on television, Atticus said, "Guess what."

"What?" I asked.

He answered, "I loved you before I was ever born."

***

Journal Entry
April 2016
8 Years 8 Months

I repeatedly have to tell Atticus what to do day in and day out. His brain never seems to focus long enough to remember to do anything on his own. It's tiring for me, and, I believe, he sees me as more of a drill sergeant than a mother at times.

This evening, I was trying to get him to take a shower. I had to tell him several times to go upstairs. Once upstairs, I had to tell him several times to take off his clothes. I was constantly shouting out commands as usual. Then Atticus said, "I'm getting tired of you bossing me around."

I said, "Then start doing things you know you're supposed to do before I have to tell you to do them."

He just stood there, naked, looking at me. I stood there looking at him, hoping he would get in the shower without me saying another word.

We continued to stare at each other while the shower water wasted away in the background.

I finally broke the silence and shouted more commands, "Check the water to see if it's too hot, too cold, or just right, then get in the shower." I paused, and then I said, "See, I still have to tell you what to do."

He laughed and hopped in the shower.

***

Journal Entry
April 2016
8 Years 8 Months

Atticus was preparing to leave with his dad when he stopped to give me a hug and kiss. As I was hugging him, he said, "You're filling me up with love. You're filling me up with so much love. My heart grows bigger every day."

How can I not adore this boy?

***

Journal Entry

May 2016

8 Years 9 Months

While preparing Atticus for bed tonight, he asked, "Did I ever injure you?"

"Yes," I told him without thinking, "I gave birth to you. I was sore for weeks."

"Did you have blood coming out of your belly?"

His question confused me. "Blood coming out of my belly?"

"Yeah, when you gave birth to me," he said.

Concerned where this conversation was heading, I replied, "No. I had blood coming out of somewhere else"

"Lots and lots of blood?" he asked.

"Yes. Lots and lots of blood. Giving birth is bloody business."

Atticus crinkled his nose, vigorously shook his head, and said, "Ugh! I'm so glad I'm not a girl!"

***

Journal Entry

June 2016

8 Years 10 Months

Atticus and I were discussing the differences between boys and girls tonight. I told him that he's all boy. I presented my proof by telling him he likes disgusting things, he picks his nose, and he has a disturbing sense of humor. Then I said, "You're all boy. Plus, you have a wee-wee willy."

He said, "Penis. Boys have a penis, and girls have some other private part."

I said, "Yes, boys have a penis and girls have a…" I paused, wondering whether it was a good idea to tell him what a girl has.

Before I could decide what to say, Atticus said, "Girls have an anti-penis!"

***

Journal Entry

Hello, My Name Is Awesome

August 2016

A Few Days Shy of 9 Years Old

Atticus is currently obsessed with television ratings. His idea of a good time is taking real-life events and deciding what rating they should receive: G, PG, TV14, MA. Should the events have an extra designation of V, S, D, or L? Whatever the situation, you can always count on Atticus to relate everything to a television rating these days.

He was with his dad this afternoon and broke his forearm when he jumped off a rock wall. When I arrived at the hospital, I talked with the doctors and told them about Atticus's anxiety, sensitivity to touch, and advised that he probably wouldn't be cooperative when they reset and put a cast on his arm. The doctors decided to sedate him for the procedure.

The room was overflowing with doctors and nurses while they were preparing Atticus for sedation. Every single professional was patient and kind except for the one responsible for putting the needle in his arm.

Atticus was freaking out about the needle, and the male nurse grew more frustrated by the moment. He harshly raised his voice when addressing Atticus, which made Atticus less sure of the situation and less cooperative. Fortunately, a warm and friendly female nurse stepped in and was able to calm Atticus in the moment. Once their conversation was complete, Atticus told the audience of doctors and nurses that he needed to pray before he could continue.

Each person paused as Atticus bowed his head and prayed for courage and safety in the name of Jesus. Amen.

The nurse was then able to insert the needle into Atticus's arm without issue. Once the sedative was flowing, a nurse escorted Tim and me to the waiting room while the medical staff put Atticus's arm back together.

Upon our return, we found a chatty, but clearly under the influence Atticus, and two unfamiliar nurses. Nurse Joe said when our son woke up, he told them all about his adventures flying through space with Darth Vader—who happened to be Nurse Joe in his dream. Atticus and Darth traveled on a spaceship and visited every planet in our solar system—including Pluto. Nurse Joe and Atticus debated whether Pluto was a planet as the discussion of space continued.

After a while, the medical personnel concluded Atticus was ready to go home. They helped him get into a wheelchair, and a nurse pushed him down the hallway. Tim and I followed with two other nurses. We were all heading toward the exit when Atticus randomly said, "I would rate my day PGDS."

One of the nurses asked, "What does the 'DS' stand for."

Atticus replied, "Drama and suspense."

The adults laughed, and one of the nurses chuckled that he had certainly had a lot of that today.

Atticus then said, "And maybe an L rating. But that won't stand for language, it will stand for laughter."

***

And that's the thing about Atticus. Despite an autism diagnosis, and the struggles that accompany it, he has provided an enormous supply of laughter throughout the years, which has sustained me through some of my darkest moments. He is the most kind, gentle, loving, caring human being I've ever encountered, and mothering him has taught me more about myself than I ever cared to learn.

Life with Atticus has been an unexpected but awesome experience designed and guided by our Creator. When I think back on our early years together, when I wasn't sure if I was capable of mothering such a unique and fascinating child, I picture God on His throne laughing along with me. As He looks down, He smiles and watches over our lifelong adventure together. Then He softly whispers in my ear, "See, you were perfect for each other after all."

End

www.ingramcontent.com/pod-product-compliance
Lightning Source LLC
Chambersburg PA
CBHW070818160726
48004CB00001B/328